SHORT CUTS TO DESIGNER STYLE

Decorative Effects

SHORT CUTS TO DESIGNER STYLE

Decorative Effects

JO AVISON

WARD LOCK

A WARD LOCK BOOK
First published in the UK 1997
by Ward Lock
Wellington House
125 Strand
LONDON
WC2R 0BB

A Cassell Imprint

First paperback edition 1998

Distributed in the United States
by Sterling Publishing Co., Inc.
387 Park Avenue South, New York, NY 10016-8810

A British Library Cataloguing in Publication Data block for this book may be obtained from the British Library

ISBN 0 7063 7739 7

Designed by Les Dominey
Jacket design by Fielding Rowinski
Jacket photograph by Osborne Little
Illustrations by Valerie Hill
Printed and bound in Spain

ACKNOWLEDGEMENTS

With special gratitude to Malcom and to Angie for their unfailing commitment and support, and my warmest appreciation to Billy Neville, of Poupette Interiors, for imparting his wonderful skills and sharing so many of his best-kept trade secrets.
Also heartfelt thanks to Helen Denholm, Rosemary Anderson, Esther Jagger, Les Dominey and Valerie Hill, for ther beautiful illustrations throughout this series.
My thanks to everyone else involved for their help and hard work in producing this book. A last, special word to my sister Caroline for her helpful contritubion, to my friends for their enthusiasm and to Ben for his continued patience

Contents

Introduction

The way in which a room is decorated goes beyond choosing a colour scheme or a wallpaper design. The overall style or shape of the room provides the framework, and your taste and the purpose of the room combine to create the kind of atmosphere you want. You can then choose the colours or papers or methods of decoration to fit within those parameters. There is so much you can do to affect the atmosphere you want to create, that choosing a style and scheme can often take as long as the decorating itself.

The scope is endless and you can go to the extent of transforming a room completely depending on the decorative effects you choose, working within the size and style limits of the room itself. For example, a room with low ceilings and box-like proportions can be decorated to mimic the style of a Mediterranean apartment with colour-washed walls and bleached wood or tiled floors and cobalt blues or terracotta fabrics. Alternatively, the same shape can lend itself to a cottage-style finish, where flower borders or hand-painted stencils make a cosy, homely atmosphere. The addition of a picture rail and the use of some clever paint effects will produce a completely different look again.

It does not need to be a long and difficult process to select your style or to undertake the decorating and get professional results for yourself. This book provides a wide range of techniques, through a large number of fully illustrated projects, that can be adapted and selected for different styles and rooms. Among them are many tricks and accessible methods used by skilled decorators to get beautiful and lasting results as directly as possible.

For you to love a room it must suit your lifestyle and your budget, as well as your design taste – and if you want to do it yourself this book can help you to achieve it with ease.

1
Before You Start

In this chapter:

- Preparation
- Working with colour
- Proportion
- Inspiration

PREPARATION

The magic word when creating any paint effect or decorative scheme is preparation. Time put in at the beginning can make all the difference to whether your chosen colours and styles work together, as well as making the actual task of decorating easier. Whether you go for a special paint effect or a mixture of paint and paper, the key to making the project manageable – and to its overall success – is to put as much care and effort as possible into preparing the surfaces. Some of the techniques described in this book are in themselves very fast to execute, and a room can be transformed in no time. But without the right groundwork papers can peel off, paint effects can discolour or not adhere in the first place, and the best decorating work can bring dissatisfaction instead of delight.

It is not necessarily hard work to prepare – it is just a question of giving it the right amount of importance. Finding colour schemes, making surfaces good and mixing glazes or pasting papers can all be enjoyable and rewarding – what makes the difference is knowing what to do and the right order in which to do it. This ability comes partly from skill and experience, but a large part of it is a matter of patience,

taking time to prepare the different elements, and knowing the pitfalls to avoid.

All the projects in this book are based on the preparation detailed in Chapter 2, which describes the requirements of different surfaces for the various decorative techniques. Each project refers you to the specific kind of preparation needed. Sometimes the preparation will take longer than the effect – all that needs to be said here is that it will be worth it in the end.

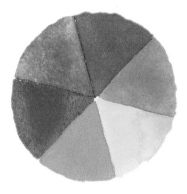

The colour wheel.

WORKING WITH COLOUR

Colour is a broad and fascinating subject. There are some basic rules that can be used as a guide, although personal taste, a little confidence and some time spent experimenting will prove the most effective tools. Colour is as much a science as an art and, without studying it in great depth, it is worth understanding some of the fundamental principles. These are best demonstrated by looking at what is known as the colour wheel.

Colour can bring vitality and drama, calm and tranquillity – it is a very important element of decoration.

Yellows and greens have the fresh quality of early spring.

Pure colours are called hues. Each hue has a tonal value that makes it a darker or lighter version, depending on whether its tone moves towards black or towards white.

Firstly, every colour has its complementary colour at the opposite position on the colour wheel. Colours are divided into primary, secondary and tertiary. The primaries are red, yellow and blue. When two of these are mixed together, you get the colour between them on the wheel – orange, green and purple, the secondary colours. Tertiaries are made up of three colours blended together.

Great care must be taken in mixing colours as too many will simply go muddy. Adding white will make a colour lighter. If you want a darker colour, it is sometimes more successful to add its opposite colour rather than black. In any case, you may not always need to mix paints – there are some very sophisticated colours available in an enormous variety of shades.

For glazes, the process of colour mixing is even more subtle and variable as the density of the colour has an effect. Glazes are translucent, and the best advice is to colour them with the appropriate artist's colours which contain strong, true pigments.

Besides the straightforward facts about colour, you will also want to take into account fashion and more intangible aspects such as emotional effects. Although there are many 'rules', each colour can be varied so much, with so many different tonal values and combinations, that it is pointless to be too rigid. Generally reds and yellows are thought to be stimulating, greens and pastels calming and relaxing, and blues and purples strong and cool. However, a purple-blue colour wash over an ivory ground, with white paintwork and soft furnishings, can look gloriously Mediterranean – as if the sun is about to burst in. Red is sometimes considered too vibrant, yet it can be darkened to a burgundy for a subdued, sophisticated appeal; and lime or apple green can be very stimulating and quite the opposite of soothing. So it would be unreasonable merely to follow the 'rules' of colour in isolation and not to consider the huge range of interpretations that are possible.

In any case, when decorating it is difficult to consider colour in isolation. Colour is, for

Red can be considered vibrant and blue cold. But they can be made to work together beautifully.

Making colours work together is one of the key aspects of successful decorative effects. Here the starkness of white is softened with a textured finish and the palest yellow ochre background to the strong blue-greens.

instance, affected by the amount of natural light in a room, and the same colour painted on walls and ceilings will look different on each plane, depending on the lighting in the room. Colour can also make a room appear larger or smaller and exert a considerable influence over the mood or atmosphere.

Bright primaries, used in contrast with each other, can be very vibrant and deliberately bold. They can give a room vitality if the right tones are used together to create a balance. Soft shades of colours from the same section of the colour wheel will blend well and be easy on the eye. If there is enough natural light to prevent

dinginess, choose purples and reds and dark orange and terracotta colours to create a darker, cosy, autumnal atmosphere; splash it with yellows for relief. Choose bright blues and yellows and paler greens to create a cool, fresh, crisp, spring effect. If a room is small, paler colours will reflect more light and make it appear larger. A large room, or one with high ceilings, will seem closer and appear smaller if it is decorated in warmer colours.

Pale shades and pastels are quite safe to work with and lend themselves well to a bold splash of contrast in a matching fabric or soft furnishings. All these aspects must be taken into

This narrow room is opened and widened with white paint and natural wood and fabric colours. A touch of gold in the material and the border lifts the room and gives a sense of more generous proportions.

consideration at the planning stage as every room needs a colour story, rather than a number of isolated choices.

A colour story, or colour schemes, are really about extending your choice of colour to include others that can all work together, whether in dynamic contrast or gentle harmony. Sometimes pattern can form another part of the same story, as mixtures of patterns in similar shades often create just the right amount of interest without adding too many different colours.

Texture can work in much the same way, providing wonderful diversity to the simplest colour schemes.

PROPORTION

This is another very important element of interior design, and one that is inextricably caught up with colour and the way it is used.

Keeping shapes in proportion can create balance in a room: you can make a narrow room look wider, a low ceiling seem higher and a dark hallway appear more bright and open. Colour can be the key to getting the proportion right.

For example, a high ceiling can be painted in quite a dark colour and the colour taken down to the picture rail. The picture rail and any decorative coving are then painted in a contrast such as white or off-white. The effect is to lower the ceiling visually. A matching dark or patterned paper or paint effect below the chair rail, with a soft, light colour in between, will balance the room and let the middle section be the main focus. This area will appear to move outwards and the darker colours will come together, giving a sense that the ceiling is lower and the room wider, rather than tall and narrow.

If you have a low ceiling, a false picture rail can be hung about 20 cm (8 in) down from the ceiling edge. Paint the ceiling in a light colour that does not form a strong contrast to the walls. To the eye, the room has a full-height picture rail and the ceiling seems higher.

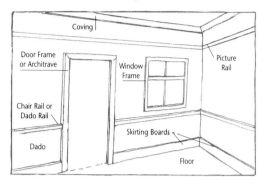

A long, narrow hall, treated with rectangular panels of wallpaper on a pale background, each panel framed with a matching contrast border, will look more interesting and less like a tunnel. A small room, treated to the same soft paint effect on walls, ceiling, radiators, doors and other woodwork, will appear bigger. If these elements were treated differently the contrasts might crowd in and increase visual competition within the small space. A gentle all-over effect that appears to recede into the background will create a sense of spaciousness. This can be added to by your choice of colour.

INSPIRATION

Colour schemes, styles and decorative techniques can be inspired from all sorts of things in your everyday surroundings. Jars of sweets in a confectioner's shop, a day by the beach, the back garden or the countryside all provide their own sources of colour and sometimes line. Another source may be a particular theme or period in architectural history that will suggest a colour and style. In every case time spent leafing through books and magazines and keeping a small scrapbook of your favourites will pay dividends in terms of how much you enjoy the finished result.

Take a pile of coloured pencils, pick your favourites and see which ones you like together.

Visit a shop that sells ready-made stencil patterns and see which of them excite you. Or you may love a particular picture postcard: a Greek island, for instance, that reminds you of blue-green seas and white buildings, or the coast of Brittany and its azure skies and glorious balconies of red geraniums. Play with ideas in your scrapbook and hone down the choices until you are left with your favourites. Go to a fabric shop and ask for swatches, or leaf through magazines and catalogues and cut out the things that attract you. You will gradually start to see a style emerging, and be able to choose the best decorative styles to experiment with.

Taking your favourite colours or the themes you have chosen, play with the different paint colours and effects and practise them on lining paper, pinned to the surface you intend to decorate. It takes a certain amount of confidence to choose and create your own decorative effects – the actual doing of them is more about patience and practice. Finding your starting point is the key – and enjoy filling your scrapbook!

A tall narrow room, or a small one, has its proportions changed by decorative treatment low on the wall. Here the lines are further manipulated by a delightful pattern of fish used up and around the wall.

2
Basic Techniques and Equipment

There is a huge range of tools and equipment available, especially for creating special paint effects. Once you have decided what you want to do, visit a specialist supplier to find out what is on offer and get some sound technical advice on the use of different tools.

Some pieces of equipment are essential, and all these are listed below. One or two can be improvised – for instance, a plumbline can be made from a length of twine with a padlock tied to it. However, in some areas good tools are crucial to the result – brushes are a good example. Although quality brushes may seem expensive, it is worth paying the extra to avoid them shedding their bristles and to get good coverage. Turn to p. 21 to discover how to keep your brushes in good condition.

This chapter gives details of the equipment required for working with both paint and paper. It also covers, step by step, the necessary preparation before you embark on either of these. If your chosen decorative scheme includes both painting and papering, then the preparation

In this chapter:
- General equipment
- Equipment for preparing and repairing surfaces
- Equipment for painting and special effects
- Paint, glaze and varnish
- Equipment for papering
- Care and cleaning of equipment
- Making good the surfaces
- Preparing surfaces for decoration
- Painting solid colour
- Types of glaze for special paint effects
- Preparing for papering
- Cutting and pasting paper

requirements apply throughout. You can then treat the areas to be painted as one project and the areas to be papered as another. In this situation the painting is usually undertaken before the papering.

Plan what you want to do in advance and make sure you have all the necessary equipment to hand. Prepare rooms thoroughly, covering carpets, clearing furniture out of the way wherever possible, and, if necessary, covering it completely with dust sheets. It is sometimes helpful to use both polythene and fabric dust sheets, particularly if you are trying to protect beautiful fabrics. Polythene underneath will prevent spilt paint seeping through a fabric dust sheet, while the fabric cover holds the polythene one in place.

Alternative methods and materials to those described here can often be used to equal effect. But the basic techniques given in these pages have been tried, tested and proven in the day-to-day world of the craftsman decorator: they have been selected for their reliability as simple, direct ways of achieving good results and professional decorative finishes.

GENERAL EQUIPMENT

RAGS: For cleaning and lifting off minor errors – have plenty.

DUST SHEETS: For covering furniture and carpets.

PENCILS: Use HB pencils to mark up walls. Ballpoint will show through even after painting.

MASKING TAPE: For masking edges where cutting in (see p. 28) is required from carpet to skirting board etc.

PLUMBLINE: Essential for finding true verticals. You can make one from a length of string and a hanging weight such as a heavy key or a padlock.

METRE STICK: The best edge for cutting against is a tailor's metal metre stick and a small 30 cm (12 in) metal ruler for corners.

SPIRIT LEVEL: This is a wooden batten with a spirit level set at the centre, and is used for marking up horizontal lines.

LINING PAPER: This is an essential for experimenting with paint colours and effects. It also needs to be hung like wallpaper where a wall surface is too poor to work on direct.

EXTENSION ARM: Extensions for rollers to reach high up walls and on to ceilings.

LADDERS: The number and size of ladders depends on the height you need to reach. It is invariably useful to have a small pair of steps as well as a large pair.

TRESTLE: This is basically a plank or board supported at each end by a step ladder. It enables you to work along a stretch of wall without climbing up and down to move the steps. It tends to get in the way of wallpapering, but can be extremely useful when painting and cutting in (see p. 28).

KITCHEN PAPER: This is needed for cleaning up and 'rescuing', as well as for blotting up excess colour on paint effects that need to be applied with a dry brush.

APRON WITH POCKETS: It is essential to have your tools actually with you, particularly when at the top of a ladder.

DUSTING BRUSH: Something you need with you all the time.

There are many different tools for the range of decorating techniques. Some use specialist equipment while others rely on household objects from vegetables to dustbin liners – whatever will make an attractive mark in a glaze.

EQUIPMENT FOR PREPARING AND REPAIRING SURFACES

SUGAR SOAP: Cleans painted surfaces and must be rinsed well. It is essential to use sugar soap or your paint will not adhere. There are many proprietary brands.

STRIPPING SOLUTIONS: Available as paint or paper strippers. Follow manufacturer's instructions for use.

HOT AIR STRIPPER: Like a hair dryer for stripping paint, and much safer than a blowtorch in certain conditions.

STEAMER: Used for removing large areas of wallpaper, and available for hire from most DIY stores.

ELECTRIC SANDER: This is very useful if you are preparing large areas, as it reduces the time and effort required.

SANDING BLOCK: A wooden block wrapped in sandpaper or wet and dry paper, for rubbing down and keying surfaces.

SANDPAPER AND WET AND DRY PAPER: Various grades of sandpaper – or wet and dry – are required for different surfaces and purposes.

SCRAPERS: Rigid scrapers are used to remove soaked paper and paint.

CHISEL OR OLD SCREWDRIVER: Ideal for routing out any cracks before filling.

FILLER: Standard and fine fillers are used for walls and woodwork respectively.

FLEXIBLE SCRAPER: Tool used for spreading filler.

Preparation is the magic word in any decorative effects – they will only be enhanced by time spent making a sound foundation.

HINT
Once you have put sufficient glaze for one wall into a paint tray, cover the glaze tightly with clingfilm or a lid. White spirit will evaporate while you work, and this will cause your perfect-consistency glaze to go thick.
(If it does thicken, add white spirit in very small amounts at a time.)

PAINT, GLAZE AND VARNISH

Details of the right paints and glazes are given for each project in the chapters.

EMULSION PAINT: Water-based paints are very easy to apply and are designed primarily for covering large areas such as walls and ceilings. Because they are water-based they are absorbed easily, so certain surfaces such as new plaster must be treated first (see p. 22). Emulsion is available in matt (for ceilings) and vinyl silk (for walls). Vinyl silk is particularly appropriate for painting bathrooms and kitchens where steam or water are present. Matt paint tends to bruise more easily and is harder to clean.
As emulsions are water-based, brushes, rollers and kettles can be cleaned in warm water and washing-up liquid.

OIL-BOUND PAINTS: These are available in eggshell, which gives a mid-sheen finish, and gloss, which has a shine. They are used on walls in certain situations and are the type required for painting woodwork and furniture. Today, while gloss is mandatory for any outdoor work, eggshell finish has become very popular for indoor painting. It is just as tough and hard-wearing as gloss and is also the perfect base on walls and ceilings for most special paint effects. Oil-bound paint requires an undercoat. However it is perfectly acceptable, and usually more economical, to apply two coats of eggshell instead of buying a separate undercoat. Brushes and tools must be cleaned in white spirit.

GLAZE: For special paint effects, the glazes or final colour washes are either oil-bound or water-based. The oil-bound variety are diluted with white spirit and the colour tint is best taken from the large selection of artist's oil colours at your local art supplier. For a water-based wash, emulsion paint is used very diluted and tinted with artist's gouache or artist's acrylics from an art supplier.

SCUMBLE: This is a special proprietary product for making a good oil-bound glaze. Sometimes called Scumble Glaze or Luxine Glaze, it contains driers and oils that make the solution workable for various paint effects.

EQUIPMENT FOR PAINTING AND SPECIAL EFFECTS

Paint Kettles: If you are working with a brush, it is much easier and safer to pour paint into a kettle than to carry the paint can around.

Paint Tray: To hold the paint if you are working with a roller.

Brushes: Household brush for general painting of large areas. Use the best quality you can afford and the size you are most comfortable with. Keep brushes separate, so that those you have used for emulsion or gloss or varnishing are retained for the same purpose. **Fitch brush:** this is a small flat brush for painting all the difficult little bits such as sharp internal corners, between radiator pipes and so on. **Radiator brush:** this is usually a standard 2.5 cm (1 in) head paintbrush attached to a flexible metal handle, which can be bent to any angle in order to access difficult areas. **Specialist brushes:** these include brushes for stencilling, stippling and dragging, besides wallpaper brushes that can also be used for special paint effects. They come in various sizes depending on the finish you want to create. There are also several types of fine brushes available for very detailed decoration.

Rollers: Come in a range of sizes and several different materials. There are sheepskin for emulsion (which do not splash like sponge), nylon and sponge varieties for different types of paint. Rollers can also be used very successfully for putting on glazes for special paint effects and for pasting wallpaper. Disposable heads are available for oil-bound paint, which is by far the easiest

alternative. Specialist rollers can roll a pattern into a glaze or on to a base coat. Plain rollers can also be tied with rags to create special effects.

Sponges: Decorators' sponges consist of a synthetic block of material backed with a plastic handle that enables you to 'spread' emulsion paint on to a wall or ceiling from a paint tray. Natural, or marine, sponges are usually used in special paint effects for sponging on and off. Household synthetic sponges give a quite different and more uniform effect, and can be cut out in different shapes for stamping.

Combs: These come in a range of materials and cut shapes and are mostly used for special effects such as graining.

Cloths: Cotton stockingette is used for some special paint effects, although a denser cotton or linen is preferable for rag rolling.

Jam Jars: Wide-necked ones are especially useful for mixing glazes. Keep the lids for safety.

Stencilling Equipment: Some specialist equipment is required for stencilling, and it is described in Chapter 5.

White Spirit: This is the main cleaning agent for oil-bound paints and varnish, and is also used to dilute them for special paint effects. Any rags that have white spirit on them must be allowed to dry flat before being thrown away, as they can be highly inflammable if stored in a confined space such as a plastic bag.

LINSEED OIL: This is added to the oil-bound glaze that is used in most special paint effects. It must be used very carefully and sparingly because too much applied to a wall will react to light changes and go yellow, causing uneven discoloration some time after the painting is finished.

PAINT STRIPPER: This is a chemical solution designed to dissolve old oil-bound paint and must be used exactly according to the manufacturer's instructions on the container.

MASKING TAPE: Stick to the edges of carpets etc. to avoid paint overlaps.

EQUIPMENT FOR PAPERING

PASTING TABLE: This is an essential piece of equipment for papering and folds away easily after use. See p. 34 for details of how to prepare the pasting table.

LINING PAPER: Used to cover the pasting table, to protect wall coverings and also to line walls where the surface is imperfect or the wallpaper requires backing. Walls can be lined as a foundation for painting and paint effects.

BUCKET: For mixing the paste.

PAINT TRAY AND NYLON ROLLER: When hanging paper, it is much easier and faster to apply paste with a nylon roller from a paint tray than with a brush.

WALLPAPER PASTE: Available in flakes or powder, it is mixed with water to the appropriate dilution for the weight of paper being hung.

BORDER ADHESIVE: Normal wallpaper adhesive may be used when applying borders to walls or paper coverings. However, on vinyls use either special border adhesive or vinyl overlap adhesive.

SMALL PASTING BRUSH: This is a 1.25 cm (½ in) household brush for touching in edges and corners that have dried slightly or might have been missed.

PLASTIC SPATULA: This wonderful piece of equipment takes the place of a wallpaper brush or seam roller. (Seam rollers tend to press the wallpaper at the seams and bruise it slightly, causing a sheen over the joins which can highlight the very line you are trying to disguise.) A 30 cm (12 in) plastic spatula or scraper with a bevelled edge allows you to press the wallpaper gently into place with a brushing motion, and naturally includes the seam without over-emphasising it. It also makes for even adhesion, as the paste is well spread as you work.

SYNTHETIC SPONGE: Ideal for wiping away excess paste that has seeped out at the edges and for washing over newly hung paper.

STRAIGHT-BLADED KNIFE WITH SNAP-OFF BLADES: This is an essential piece of equipment for cutting in and getting crisp edges when hanging paper. The snap-off blades are important as you must always work with a very sharp knife.

15 CM (6 IN) SCRAPER: This is a rigid scraper that is used as a guide for cutting in.

METAL STRAIGHT EDGE: This provides the line against which you use the knife for clean, perfect edges.

EXPANDING METAL TAPE MEASURE: For measuring drops and measuring up wallpaper. Better than a cloth measure, which may stretch.

PENCIL: For marking up wallpaper. Never use ballpoint.

DECORATORS' SCISSORS: These are for cutting wallpaper and snipping it to fit around obstructions such as light fittings. A knife is not so easy to use for such tasks and may damage fittings.

PLUMBLINE AND BOB: Essential for checking as you work that the drops of wallpaper are hung straight. You can use a spirit level, but a plumbline is often more accurate and easier to use.

CARE AND CLEANING OF EQUIPMENT

In all decorating it is crucial to keep the surfaces, the materials, the tools and yourself as clean as possible to avoid spoiling your work. Brushes with a residue of paint in them will give you three problems. They will not brush efficiently if paint has dried in the stock (bristles). They may discolour the new paint. And if any emulsion is left in the stock of a brush that is later used for oil-bound paint the emulsion will 'peel out'; this means that tiny nibs of it will come out in the gloss or eggshell as you work.

Rollers and brushes, rags and sponges that have been used for emulsion all need to be thoroughly washed out in warm water containing plenty of washing-up liquid. Equipment that has been used for oil-bound paint must be thoroughly cleaned in white spirit and then washed with plenty of warm water and washing-up liquid. This is essential for expensive specialist brushes such as those used for stippling or stencilling.

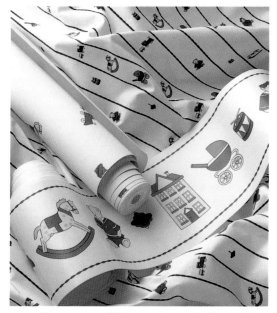

Matching papers and fabrics, and using borders to link soft furnishings together, is part of the fun of creating decorative effects. Filling your scrapbook is invariably time well spent.

> ### HINT
> Paint strippers and other decorating materials and equipment are often toxic and/or inflammable. Keep babies, children and pets away from all areas being decorated until the work is finished and dry. Chemicals used for stripping are usually poisonous, so always read and follow the manufacturer's instructions and work in a well-ventilated room or outside if possible, wearing a mask and protective gloves wherever advised. Keep all aerosols away from heat and do not puncture even when empty.

Dry brushes thoroughly, oil them lightly with linseed oil to preserve their softness, then hang up or store them bristles upward.

If you are using rollers with oil-bound paint it is best to go for the disposable variety. Rollers used with water-based paint can be washed out like brushes. Sponges are cleaned in the same way as brushes, although they do need replacing fairly regularly. Varnish must be washed out with white spirit only. Rags soaked in white spirit, either to clean other tools or in the creation of a paint finish, must be left to dry completely in the air before they are disposed of – they can be highly inflammable when stored in confined spaces such as plastic waste bags.

Before storing paint or varnish, clean around the lid and make sure it is securely closed (use a hammer, if necessary, to get the lid fully and evenly down). If paint has gone lumpy or formed a skin, you can strain it through a piece of stockingette or an old pair of tights.

> ### HINT
> Always use warm water, not hot, when cleaning equipment used with emulsion paint. Hot water causes emulsion to solidify, making it difficult to clean off. Also, brushes used for oil-bound paint, even after soaking in white spirit should be cleaned in warm, not hot, water.

MAKING GOOD THE SURFACES

A good foundation will make your special paint effect or papering much easier to do. Indeed, a poor foundation can destroy the whole effect – watching paper fall off inadequately prepared walls or patches of glaze go dull where the base was not covered, can be soul-destroying.

Different surfaces require different preparatory treatments, which depend to some extent on what you intend to do later. Some paint effects work on emulsion, while others need oil-bound bases. Wallpaper requires a different preparation from paint, and so does lining paper – this is often hung as a backing to wallpaper or to give a sound surface for the paint effect. Below are some of the types of surface you may encounter and details of how to prepare them for painting, papering and special paint effects.

WALLS AND CEILINGS:

Old or painted walls should be washed down with sugar soap solution, then rinsed off and allowed to dry. Rout out any cracks with a screwdriver or blunt chisel and dampen the edges of cracks and pits before filling them with proprietary filler. Over-fill slightly so that you can sand back after the filler has dried. Remake chipped external corners and repair internal corners using your finger or a flexible filler knife.

When sanding the dried walls, make sure they are as flat as possible – take care to flatten patches of filler. Use sandpaper on a block for this stage. Feel with your hand to check that the surface is smooth, and brush off or vacuum up the sanding dust afterwards. Hiring a power sander is a great time-saver for large expanses of wall.

New walls, or new plaster, need four to six weeks, according to the temperature and conditions, to dry out fully. They may still tend to crack a little, so, although they can be painted in the meantime, they should not be papered. Any new plaster needs to be sealed. Because of its propensity for absorption you must apply a 'mist coat' of paint before emulsioning a new wall. This is a very thin coat of emulsion paint, diluted 50:50 with water. Cover the wall completely in this mist coat and let it dry. If the mist coat is not applied, the water in the emulsion paint will be absorbed rapidly into the plaster wall and the paint will soon start to peel off.

Papered walls, and the question of whether or not to strip them, depends on what you intend to do afterwards. You can paint directly on to many matt-surfaced wallpapers. In this case check that the surface is even, that the paper is stuck down anywhere it may be lifting, such as at the seams, and that any tears or missing pieces are repaired.

If the paper is vinyl, or if you intend to paper or paint directly on to the wall surface, then the wall needs to be stripped. It is claimed that some vinyl wall coverings can be stripped off in two layers, so that you can remove the top layer and leave the backing paper underneath as a lining if you wish. In practice this is rarely advisable, as you are wholly dependent on how well the paper was hung and on the even adhesion of the original paste. What can happen is that the new paper will be fine when it first goes up and sticks to the backing paper. But some time later, wherever the underneath paper comes unstuck the extra weight will bring old and new paper off together. You are usually better off taking the time to strip it.

Soak the wall with hot water containing a liberal amount of washing-up liquid and strip the wallpaper off with a rigid metal scraper. Alternatively hire a steamer for the purpose. Remove all the paper and then treat the wall as for painted surfaces, sanding it smooth and wiping away the sanding dust.

Plasterboard walls must be dry stripped, as plasterboard will not tolerate extensive wetting. Otherwise treat as above, sanding the surface smooth when you have finished.

The design of this room is based on a natural look for floor, furnishings, door and architrave. In keeping with this the walls have been treated with a broken colour technique to create a soft background that is gentle on the eye.

WOODWORK: This will be either new or painted. You do not generally have to strip painted wood if you intend to paint it again, but it must be thoroughly cleaned to remove any grease and then sanded to key the surface. If there is a heavy build-up of old, chipped paint which it is necessary to strip, use paint stripper and a metal scraper or else a hot air gun. In either case, follow the manufacturer's instructions carefully and take all necessary precautions.

New wood must be knotted and primed before sanding. Paint the knots with knotting solution and paint the woodwork with primer first. Fill cracks in new or old woodwork with fine surface filler. Allow to dry, then sand away any nibs until the surface is completely smooth. Where knots show through woodwork that has already been painted, treat them with knotting compound before repainting – just as if it was new wood. In this case there would be no need to prime the wood. You can repaint it after sanding.

FLOORS: These lend themselves well to being painted or to being treated with special paint effects. The type of preparation depends on the surface – and to some extent the chosen effect – as you may want to leave the floor rough as part of the finish. Most floors can be covered with hardboard to make a good firm base, or painted with a commercial floor paint that is very hard-wearing.

There is often a lot of work involved in preparing a wooden floor, even if you only want to varnish floorboards. First make sure the surface is flat and that all nails are either removed or hammered in (hiring a commercial sander will save a lot of time). Press papier mâché – a mulch of wallpaper glue and shredded newspaper – into gaps between floorboards if they are not new, in order to cork the seams. The wood can be varnished in matt or gloss or – if it is to be painted – knotted (if new), primed and undercoated; you can then paint two coats of eggshell paint over the undercoat. For added protection – particularly if you have applied stencils – the eggshell can be finished with matt or gloss varnish.

PREPARING THE SURFACES FOR DECORATION

PREPARING THE SURFACE FOR PAINTING: Once the surfaces have been made good they are ready to receive paint. The type of paint you choose will depend to some extent on what you intend to do ultimately. Plain painting of walls and ceilings is usually done in emulsion, as it can be applied quickly and easily with a roller over large areas. This is the perfect surface for sponging (see p. 56), some stencilling and any adaptations you may choose to do in a water-based finish.

The majority of the special effects, however, have an oil-bound base which is designed to support the type of glaze recommended in this book (see below).

Woodwork is painted in oil-bound paint, either gloss or eggshell. While gloss is mandatory for outdoor work, indoor work is often more attractive in the less shiny finish.

PREPARING THE SURFACE FOR PAPERING: Once the surface is smooth and ready it is good practice to size it if you intend to hang wallpaper or lining paper. This will give the surface uniform adhesion properties. It will also seal in all the fine dust left after sanding. Watch out particularly for old distempered walls. Paper will not stick to them, so in this case it is essential to seal the surface by sizing it.

Make a weak solution of proprietary bonding agent by mixing it with five times the amount of water, and apply it with a large household brush. Be sure to cover the whole surface. Sizing is also essential on new plaster: if you leave out this stage, paper will adhere initially but come off some time later.

PREPARING THE SURFACE FOR SPECIAL PAINT EFFECTS: Glaze is used to apply most of the special paint effects. It is a very thin, diluted colour, which, when applied, will highlight any blemish or fault in the wall surface. If this is part of a very informal or deliberately rough-textured finish, it is not unacceptable. The base colour can be applied directly over old wallpaper or on to plaster. However, because of this characteristic of showing up faults, in many cases the preparation takes longer than the actual application of the special effect and must be done with great care.

The way to a truly professional finish on decorative paint effects is to prepare the surface as near to perfection as possible. This is particularly important with effects such as rag rolling and dragging that are to cover large areas. They must have a smooth and even depth of colour, which will be spoiled by a poorly prepared surface.

Walls and ceilings: To prepare for paint effects, either paint on to the surface directly if it is good enough, or apply lining paper. To line, make good as described above and size the wall or ceiling. Hang the lining paper vertically throughout, taking it right to the edges as if it was wallpaper (see p. 116).

Cover the lining paper with two coats of eggshell paint, using a disposable roller suitable for oil-bound paint. Make sure the lined wall is completely covered by the first coat. It will tend to fur up the lining paper, so lightly sand it away before applying the second coat. Again ensure that the wall is completely covered by the second coat, as the paint effect will reveal any uneven coverage after it has dried.

One way to avoid this problem is to tint the paint used for the undercoat with a very tiny amount of universal stainer. Pour off some paint into a paint kettle and mix in the stainer – just enough to make a slight shade difference so that you can see clearly when you have covered that first coat completely.

If you are going to paint directly on to a plain or painted surface, then make sure that the base is completely covered by the eggshell undercoat and the undercoat completely covered by the top coat. Otherwise it will show through the paint effect and spoil the way the glaze works, preventing it from adhering properly.

Woodwork is prepared as above, in the same way as for plain painting. You require the same two coats – one undercoat and one top coat – of eggshell paint. Always let the undercoat dry completely, and then sand it smooth before applying the top coat. This is especially important when applying a special paint effect as the glaze will highlight any imperfections.

Metalwork such as furniture and metal windows is best stripped and rubbed down with wire wool to remove grime and/or rust. Prime with metal primer and paint with two coats of eggshell. If you have a lot of metal windows it is often worth having them professionally stripped as this is a long and tedious job. For metal furniture, consider using enamel spray paints (see Chapter 5), which are specifically designed for metal and come in a wide range of colours and finishes.

PAINTING SOLID COLOUR

Painting plain colour is the easiest and fastest decorative option of all. The best short cut, as ever, is good preparation. With the right equipment and paint, and a smooth foundation, you can fly along painting walls, ceilings, woodwork and furniture beautifully.

WALLS AND CEILINGS: These are usually painted in water-based emulsion paint as it is so quick and easy to apply. Some special paint effects are the exception, as these usually need an oil-bound base (see p. 24). In either case the technique for covering a large area is the same.

Wherever possible use a roller, as it is much faster than a brush. Use the roller first over the main expanse and then, while the edge of the rolled paint is still wet, cut into the corners, edges and coving with a brush.

Always work your roller in every possible direction as you go. Otherwise you will get an effect called 'planking', in which the roller tends to create lines as you work it up and down. Emulsion dries relatively quickly, and must be allowed to do so before applying the next coat.

Except when using commercial paints that are designed to be applied in one coat only, always paint at least two coats of emulsion to surfaces being decorated. It gives a solid base and avoids the patches and shadows that result from insufficient layers.

WOODWORK AND RADIATORS: Always use the largest brush compatible with the surface being painted, and with your own 'comfort zone'.

Having prepared the surface, take a small 2.5 cm (1 in) paintbrush (5 cm/2in if it is a wide skirting or door) and apply a coat of undercoat. Remember to apply undercoat as carefully as you would top coat.

Once the undercoat is dry, sand and dust it off before applying a single top coat – feel with one hand and sand with the other until it is nib-free and smooth. Paint the top coat carefully, letting the brush do the work. As a general rule,

paint in the direction of the wood grain. For radiators, paint in the direction of the indents or metal tubing.

DOORS: These are slightly different from other woodwork as there is an order that works best on a panelled door and a way of working that keeps a plain door smooth.

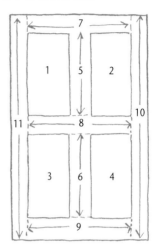

Paint a panelled door in the sequence shown here.

Paint a door with either a roller or a brush. If you are using a roller it will give an 'orange peel' finish, so brush out the paint afterwards. This is known as 'dressing' the door.

Painting a flush door with first a roller, then a brush.

Solid colour can look wonderful, and it does not have to be flat. A textured wall surface can create warmth and depth with a single-colour matt finish.

Alternatively you can use just the brush. In this case visualise the door as being made up of squares. Place your loaded brush always in the middle of each square and brush in all different directions. Then 'dress' the door as above, using vertical brush strokes. This technique ensures an even, run-free coat over the whole door.

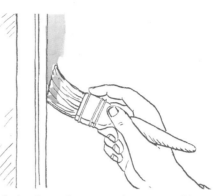

Dip the brush into the paint so that it is coated but not dripping. Push the brush against the surface, near to the edge but not on it, so that the stock forms a blade of bristles. You can then run this 'blade' right along the edge you are cutting in.

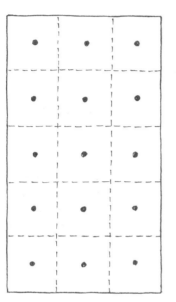

Painting a flush door with a brush only. Imagine the door is divided as shown, and work from the centre of each square.

Release the brush to paint a strip alongside the cut-in edge, forming a painted border on to which your roller or larger brush can overlap.

CUTTING IN: This technique is an important element of working with paint as it provides a neat edge where the colours change, and gives the entire decoration a professional finish if it is properly done. Cutting in is often required around window frames and door architraves, along skirting boards and along the edge of coving.

You will need two brushes – one 5 cm (2 in) household brush and one 1 cm (½ in) fitch or artist's brush. Even if you are using a roller, you cut in around the edges with these two brushes to form a border of paint which the roller can overlap without going too close to the edge.

Internal corners cannot be done as well with a larger brush, so the fitch or artist's brush is used for these.

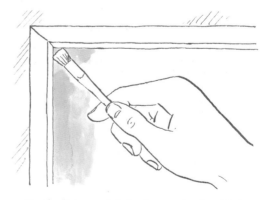

Use the fitch or artist's brush to work paint right into the corner. You can then continue the line using the larger brush.

TYPES OF GLAZE FOR SPECIAL PAINT EFFECTS

There are a huge number of special paint effects. In the most popular of them, known as broken colour techniques, a layer of paint is first applied to the wall in the base colour and then one or more layers of glaze are painted over it. Glaze is a much-thinned colour that is applied in layers, tending to be translucent rather than opaque, like flat paint. This glaze is then lifted off while it is wet and, depending on the tools used and the method applied, different effects are created. The other main method is to apply colour on to the wall using different tools and methods of application. This can be done with solid paint. However, using a glaze in this way is another successful and versatile means of creating stunning effects.

One of the things you need to understand about special paint effects is that you must not be too precious about the accuracy of detailed work. When you stand back from a wall or room decorated in a broken colour technique, detail is lost to some extent; also, minor blemishes tend to enhance the informality of the style, rather than detract from it. If the foundation is good, you will have lots of scope in the actual work. Furthermore, the addition of pictures, lamps, furniture, curtains and so on will distribute your attention over the room as a whole, and not to minute details in the paint effect.

To this end it is very important to work with colour combinations and patterns aimed at enhancing the overall effect. For example, if a blue glaze is dragged over a yellow base coat, from any distance over 60 cm–1m (2–3 ft) the wall will just appear to be a greenish colour. Experiment with paint and glaze colours before you start, and choose schemes for their compatibility as much as for their individual qualities. Work with themes that go with your

Glazes have a translucency that creates light and texture all at once. They can be applied very diluted, or darkened with oil colour for a more dramatic finish.

fabrics and furniture as well as with the shape of the room to be painted. Remember when you try out colour combinations on lining paper or a prepared board to hang it on the wall and stand back. You will probably be quite surprised at the different and often unexpected effects you can get.

Finally, never forget that a real mess is best wiped off. Minor blemishes can often be stippled out with a clean dry brush, but attempting to repair broken colour techniques extensively is usually disastrous. Put it down to experience and just start again.

There are two main ways of using glazes. The glaze itself – and the base it is painted on – can be water-based. In this case both base colour and glaze are emulsion paint, though the paint for the glaze is considerably watered down and tinted with artist's gouache or acrylic. Alternatively the whole process can be oil-based, using eggshell paint as the base colour. The glaze is then made from scumble, diluted with white spirit and tinted with artist's oil colour or universal stainers. The two types can be mixed, using oil glaze on emulsion; however, this is not the most straightforward way to work. It is often suggested that the choice between these methods is merely a matter of personal preference, but that is not really true.

The water-based method is fine for certain effects, such as sponging. It can, however, be much harder to work with on other effects because the paint dries so quickly, and it does not give the same vibrancy and response to the brush or cloth marks. The intensity of colour can also be lost in emulsion paint, and the patchy way the paint dries and its facility for absorbing water may jeopardise the results.

In practice professionals use simple techniques to create the wonderful translucency of a real glaze on oil-bound paint. They exploit tools and colour combinations for fabulous results and keep the process as compatible as possible.

The following method is reliable and relatively easy for both professionals and beginners, whichever paint effect you have chosen to do. It remains wet enough to stay workable for a considerable time. It is also the most forgiving as it can be wiped off, while it is wet, if you want to practise or start again. This method will give bright and immediate results, and you can have a great deal of fun perfecting the techniques you choose.

OIL-BOUND GLAZE

HINT
When glazing a whole room, work in this order. Paint one wall, then the wall opposite, then the wall adjacent to where you started the second wall, then the last one. Start with the wall that is seen the least – the one that most of the furniture has its back to, or the door wall. Working like this gives you time to practise the technique before you get to the wall that is focused on the most.

Prepare the wall as described on p. 24 and paint it in two coats of oil-bound eggshell in the colour of your choice. You can use one coat over an undercoat – however, if you miss the smallest patch it will be highlighted by the glaze and will always show through your finished paint effect. For ease, regard a second coat of eggshell paint as essential. Make sure this is completely dry before applying the glaze. The finish will be totally spoiled by a sticky base coat or ground.

MATERIALS
- Scumble
- White spirit
- Raw linseed oil
- Artist's oil colours
- 5 cm (2 in) household paintbrush
- Rags
- Paint kettle with lid, or lidded glass jar

PREPARATION: When you paint the wall in the base colour, it is always a good idea to paint a 30 cm (2 ft) square sheet of hardboard at the

same time. This makes a perfect practice sheet that can be wiped clean as you experiment with different effects. It also serves as a test board to get the consistency of the glaze right.

METHOD: Mix equal amounts of scumble and white spirit to make enough to cover the whole area. As a rough guide, 1 litre (1.75 pints) will cover all the walls of a room 4 x 5m (12 x 15 ft). Add two tablespoons of raw linseed oil to the mix. Tint with artist's oil colour, using small amounts at a time until you have the colour you want.

In a corner where it can be wiped off, or on a test board held upright, try out the glaze: make a horizontal brush mark and see if the glaze stays exactly where you put it. If it runs, you need to add more scumble. If it is too thick to show the brush marks, you need to add white spirit. Do this a little at a time, testing as you go along. The small amount of raw linseed oil helps to keep a 'wet edge' when you are working, which enables you to do larger areas at a time. If you find the glaze is drying too quickly, add a very small amount of raw linseed oil. (Do not use too much, as it may cause the glaze to go yellow in time.)

Once the glaze is the consistency and colour you require, continue by using one of the methods outlined in the following chapters. These include several basic paint effects and some of the professional short cuts to obtaining the best results as easily as possible. Remember, too, that this glaze wipes off while it is wet, so disasters can always be removed with a clean rag dampened with white spirit and you can start again.

WATER-BASED GLAZE FOR SPECIAL PAINT EFFECTS

For water-based paint effects the wall is prepared in emulsion paint, preferably vinyl silk as it is more forgiving to work on. Sponging relies on this type of paint, as it is built up in layers of different colours. It is very easy to do.

MATERIALS

- Water
- Emulsion paint, vinyl silk for preference
- Artist's acrylic or gouache colours
- 5 cm (2 in) household paintbrush
- Rags
- Paint kettle to mix in
- Saucer or polystyrene tray to hold the glaze as you work

PREPARATION: When you paint the wall in the base colour, paint a 60 cm (2 ft) square sheet of hardboard at the same time. This is the perfect practice sheet for wiping clean as you experiment with different effects and paint consistencies.

METHOD: Mix equal amounts of water and emulsion paint so that you have enough to cover the whole area. As a rough guide, 1 litre (1¾ pints) will cover all the walls of a room 4 x 5m (12 x 15 ft). Tint with artist's acrylic or gouache colour, using small amounts at a time until you have the colour you want. Pour a little into a polystyrene tray to work from.

You may need more water – up to 75 per cent – to get the right colour density. Alternatively you can use a watered down coloured emulsion paint for this effect – it is very easy to mix and use. It does not give the strength or translucency of an oil-bound glaze, but the finish is very subtle and it can be manipulated by using more or less water. The more dilute the mix, the softer the finish; the less water you use, the stronger the colour will be.

PREPARING FOR PAPERING

It is essential to plan out your papering – it makes life considerably easier and the process of papering much faster and less daunting.

MATERIALS

- Plumbline
- Small strip of your chosen wallpaper as a guide
- HB pencil

PREPARATION: Choose a wall without windows or light switches to start on – preferably one that is not the focal point of the room, such as the fireplace wall. Do that wall last when you have had some practice at handling the paper.

1. Cut an 8 cm (3 in) strip off your wallpaper roll to use as your planning guide. Take your pencil and guide and go round the room, marking at eye level where the edge of one piece of paper will meet the next. Treat each wall as a separate entity, ensuring that the first and last piece on each wall are not too skinny.

2. Check each drop for obstructions such as doors, radiators and light switches. Ideally aim for items such as light switches to be positioned where two pieces meet. Cutting around a switch is much easier than cutting through paper. For the best positioning, see the advice on papering around doorways and windows in Chapter 7.

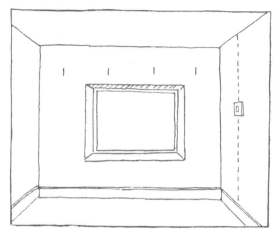

3. Stand back and assess how easy or difficult each piece of paper will be to hang. It is quite common to plan a room several times before the result is satisfactory. Choose a new height or mark for each set of marker points as you go, so that you know which ones to use finally.

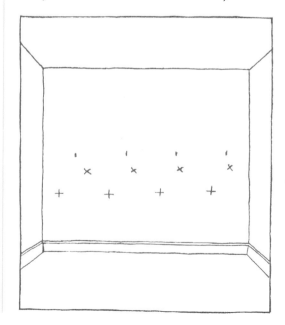

4. When you are happy, number each marker and cut one wall's worth of paper, numbering each sheet accordingly. Few rooms are square, so side pieces may be unusual shapes. A right-handed person will usually paper according to the numbers shown here, a left-handed person the opposite way.

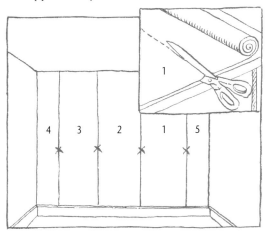

5. In terms of length, ensure you have taken into account the height of the drop plus 5 cm (2 in) top and bottom trimming allowance, plus any pattern drop (see p. 34).

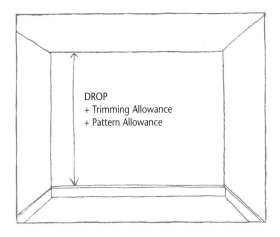

DROP
+ Trimming Allowance
+ Pattern Allowance

6. To hang your first piece of paper start at the marker on the right-hand side of piece no. 1. Take your plumbline (ensure it is at least the length of the drop) and attach or hold it at the top of the wall, so that it hangs over your marker. Working your way down, draw a vertical line of dashes about 25 cm (10 in) apart. This is your guide to make sure the first piece goes up straight, with the other pieces butted up to it.

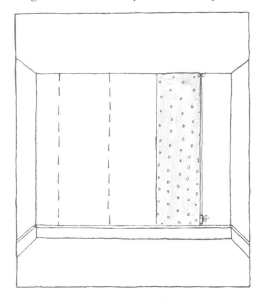

HINT
Remember that lining paper is wider than wallpaper, so if you are planning the room for hanging lining paper only (to use as a base for special paint effects, for example), use a strip of lining paper as the planning guide. If you are intending to paper over it, you must first plan with lining paper and then plan again, on the lining paper, using a strip of the actual wallpaper.

CUTTING AND PASTING PAPER

Papering requires patience; however, it is very rewarding if you take the time to do it methodically. The preparation stage is, as usual, of the utmost importance. The methods described below are tried and tested: they pre-empt some of the problems and offer a direct route to neat paper-hanging. Chapter 7 tells you how to hang the paper and how to navigate your way accurately around windows and other obstructions.

CUTTING: When you are papering, it is essential to keep everything clean to avoid getting paste anywhere other than on the back of the wallpaper. Before you start cutting, first prepare the pasting table by covering it in lining paper held down with masking tape. This will ensure that a clean surface is always presented to the decorative face of the wallpaper.

Mark out 1m (3 ft) in pencil on the lining paper on the pasting table, tagging every 10 cm (4 in). You can use this as a measuring guide for the lengths of wallpaper.

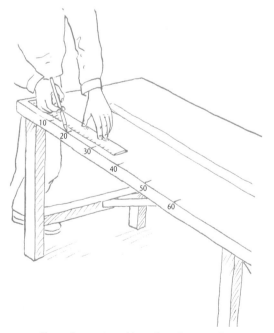

Cover the pasting table and mark up a rule.

Reverse roll the paper to minimise its tendency to curl.

Measure the drop length. That means the height of the walls or required length of the strip, plus an allowance of 5–8 cm (2–4 in) for trimming. For patterned papers, see the advice on pattern matching below.

Cut several lengths – a wall's worth – ready for pasting up (see the instructions on preparing to paper on p. 32). Wallpaper paste must be allowed to soak in for the required amount of time as stated on the package. Standard- or medium-weight wallpapers and lining papers need about five minutes. Heavy-duty wallpapers and lining papers need up to fifteen minutes.

With several lengths cut you can paste two or three pieces, so that when you have hung the first the second will be ready, and while the third is soaking you can hang the second. If you queue the drops in this way you will get into a rhythm and be able to work steadily, hanging and pasting in batches.

While paste must be taken to the edges, it is equally important not to get any on the table. To this end, draw the paper towards you to overhang the table edge by approximately 6 mm (½ in), and reverse for the opposite side.

PATTERN MATCHING: Cut the first drop, including the extra allowance, and lay it face up on the table. Align the pattern when you unroll the second piece and cut accordingly, making the usual allowance of 5–8 cm (2–4 in) as well. Some patterns have a long pattern drop, while others match at half the pattern to reduce waste.

Unroll the next piece, aligning the pattern.

WALLPAPER PASTE: All-purpose, cellulose-based paste that contains fungicides is available in powder form for standard wallpaper and lining papers. Mix it with water following the manufacturer's instructions. For heavier papers, you can use either ready-mixed heavy-duty paste, or the standard variety mixed with less water to make up a more concentrated solution. For washable wallpaper and vinyls – those hung in bathrooms and kitchens – use a fungicidal paste to prevent mould growing under the paper.

PASTING THE PAPER

MATERIALS

- Pasting table covered with lining paper (see above)
- Paste and water
- Bucket and stick
- Paint tray
- Roller with nylon head
- Clean sponge

PREPARATION: Mix the paste in the bucket according to the manufacturer's instructions for the type of paper you are hanging. Stir the paste well with the stick to remove lumps. Cover the pasting table with lining paper and masking tape as described above.

1. Pour some of the paste into a clean paint tray. Apply it with a nylon roller suitable for pasting. Start at the centre of the first piece and roll out from the middle.

2. Paste to one end of the paper to start with. Make sure you cover the area completely, particularly the edges. Overhang them slightly, as described above, to avoid pasting the table.

HINT
Boxing (step 4) ensures that the edges are pressed against each other during the soaking time to prevent drying out.

3. Fold the pasted end gently to the middle, leaving the fold soft. Paste up to the other end in the same way and fold back to the middle to meet the first section, butting the two ends together.

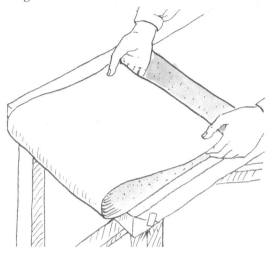

5. Cut and paste two or three drops of medium-weight paper, or three to four drops of heavy-duty paper, at the same time. Once the last piece in the batch has been pasted, the first piece will have soaked sufficiently and be ready to hang.

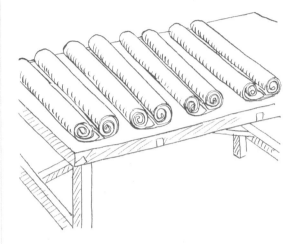

4. Starting from the fold, roll the first end gently into the middle. Then roll the second end gently into the middle until the roll looks like this. The technique is known as boxing.

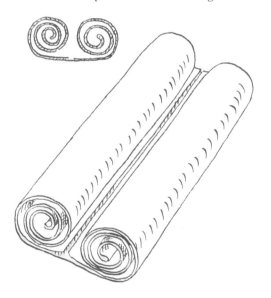

6. It is unwise to hang the folded paper over a chair or pole as is often recommended. If you do, the edges may dry out and easily become unstuck later.

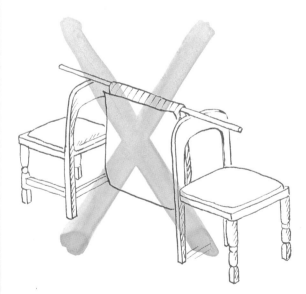

3
Special Paint Effects

There is an air of mystery surrounding special paint effects that puts many people off the idea of tackling them. Yet they can be a very easy and direct way of decorating a room or furniture, and stunning results can be achieved even by the most inexperienced beginner.

It is true that some paint effects require specialist skills and experience. Marbling and tortoiseshelling, for example – where different types of marble and tortoiseshell patterns are mimicked in paint – demand technical know-how, a skilled hand and a great deal of practice to achieve perfection. These effects, in which paint is applied to tease, if not fool, the eye into believing it really is the material being copied, are known as bravura techniques. The more elaborate ones include lapis lazuli, agate, moiré and the copying of individual bark patterns for different types of wood. In practice bravura finishes are best used where you might expect to find the real material. These beautiful treatments are often finely detailed and too time-consuming for large areas, where many of the simpler paint effects can achieve equally desirable results.

The latter offer a huge variety of decorative effects, all relatively quickly and easily achieved. Those outlined in this chapter all involve the

> **In this chapter:**
> - Colour washing
> - Rag rolling
> - Dragging
> - Stippling, shading and distressing
> - Alternative ideas

application of colour to the surface in the form of a paint glaze, which is then wiped off with a variety of tools and objects that leave a characteristic mark in the paint.

The effects of the different materials can be mixed, and the best results have as much to do with combinations of colour and treatments as with technical skill. Admittedly it helps to know whether to use oil-bound paint or water-based paint and how thin or viscous to make the glaze. Expert professional advice can reveal the tricks of the trade and help you to achieve the best results in terms of materials, timing and the order in which to work. However, it is worth taking time to experiment with colours and to practise combining the different pattern possibilities to create an effect that you can really enjoy living with.

Colour Washing

This is one of the easiest paint techniques to apply and has lots of scope in terms of both materials and colour effects. Painting a stretch of wall in solid colour can look very strong and hard, but colour washing has a translucency that gives depth and variety to the finish without necessarily losing any strength of colour.

A colour wash can be built up in layers to increase the intensity of the colour. Each coat must be allowed to dry before applying further thin layers. The wash can then be protected with a matt, mid-sheen or gloss varnish depending on the preferred finish. Gloss varnish will give a mock lacquered effect and reflect more light from the shiny surface.

Dark colour washes have a wonderful depth to them, particularly when light picks up the sheen in the glaze. Lighter colours can be used to give a room lustre, without the flatness that large areas of plain colour can have. The nature of washing is translucent and so, no matter how dark the tone, even strong colours tend not to be overpowering.

Glaze is best applied quite thinly with a throw-away sponge roller designed for oil-bound paint. The type of mark made in colour washing, as with all these paint effects, depends on the tool used to lift the glaze off. They include different-sized brushes, grasses, feathers and fabrics.

This treatment has a soft, informal style so you should use a broad, freehand stroke and avoid too regular a pattern. A wide brush, such as a wallpapering brush, will give a different effect from a dragging brush. Both of these, worked in sweeping strokes, will give a gentle texture to the colour wash. Using a cloth will give an even more subtle pattern as the thin glaze will be rubbed back and forth until the desired depth of colour is achieved. It can be added to in layers – even one colour used over another can work, if they are of similar tone and combine to enhance the theme and style of the room. This is a particularly gentle effect, as the brush marks are effectively rubbed away and some of the intensity of colour is relieved.

Colour washing is a 'large' finish in terms of the shape and size of the marks, so it is ideally suited to walls, ceilings and floors. It is harder to apply successfully to furniture, where there is rarely enough space for the sweeping strokes and easy style characteristic of the technique. It is also quite a forgiving paint effect, and does not require a perfect wall to work on. Indeed it is sometimes used deliberately to wash colour over imperfections or rough plaster, or to keep a rustic finish to the overall decor. Colour washing can also be applied over paper if the surface is suitable to absorb the paint.

Colour washing works very well combined with other techniques, particularly stencilling. Choose your colours carefully and practise combinations on some lining paper. Beautiful effects can be created by stencilling in thicker matt paint on to a colour wash of similar tone. The wash is shiny and light, and the opaque stencil motif will be subtly offset without the need of a contrast colour.

There is huge scope for combining these effects in light and dark contrasts, primaries, different pastels or matching tones. Colour washing itself can look just as stunning in the palest of shades as it can in the strongest colours, because it is so versatile and because light on the surface creates such beautiful effects. You can afford to be daring and have fun with this treatment, as it is very kind to the beginner and professional alike.

This glaze has been mixed with violet and cobalt blue, then colour washed on to an ivory base colour.
The whole room has a feel of Mediterranean skies and summer holidays.

How to Colour Wash

MATERIALS

- One paint tray per glaze to be used
- One throw-away sponge roller per glaze to be used
- Large soft wide brush
- Piece of suitable fabric if preferred to brush
- Base colour paint
- Brushes or rollers to apply base colour
- Glaze
- Small brush for corners and edges
- Plenty of dry rags or kitchen paper to clean brushes

PREPARATION

Walls need not be so well prepared for this technique, which can be so informal that damage to plaster becomes part of its character. Lining the wall is therefore optional (see p. 36). Paint two coats of eggshell paint on the surface that is to be colour washed. Wait until the second coat is dry. Then mix the glaze to the required consistency and colour, testing it first on an area that will not be seen.

TECHNIQUE

Colour washing is a relaxed, haphazard technique of making freehand brush strokes across the wall to cover it. These can be short and sharp if you like, or long and curved like grasses, going up and almost swaying over the wall in long vertical sweeps. A larger brush – even a wallpaper brush – is generally used to get the soft lines and easy grace of the colour washed mark.

Depending on the colour intensity and the effect you choose to create, you can paint with the glaze directly on to the wall, making whatever brush mark pattern appeals to you. Alternatively, for a more transparent effect roll on the glaze with a throw-away sponge roller and then take it off with a dry brush, using the same technique as dragging but with much more carefree brush strokes. Practise first, and you may find that painting the glaze directly suits the colour and style you have chosen.

HINT

It is a good idea to paint a 60 cm (2ft) square of hardboard when you apply the eggshell to the surface being treated. This becomes your test panel on which to try out colours, combinations and brush strokes before you start.

1. Pour glaze into the paint tray and roll a strip about 2 m (6 ft) wide. Do not do much more than this, as the leading edge needs to stay wet ready for the next coat to merge well.

2. Starting at one side, work up and across the wall. Using a brush or cloth, make sweeping marks up and down or criss-crossed over the glaze. Work the whole strip to within 12 cm (5 in) of the leading edge.

3. Roller another strip of glaze, working out from the still wet first strip so there are no definite lines or overlaps. You will get into a rhythm and find a natural pattern as you work.

4. Colour wash the second strip working out from the first strip so that the patterning continues in the same fashion. Avoid over-working a particular area or too much glaze will come off and leave a pale patch. Also avoid repairing small areas – it is usually better to wipe it clean and start again.

KEEPING THE BRUSH CLEAR
As soon as the brush or cloth gets too dense with glaze, wipe it dry on a rag or piece of kitchen paper. Change cloths or wipe the brush frequently. However, these requirements are less crucial in colour washing than in other glaze techniques because an uneven, haphazard effect is characteristic of the style.

APPLYING GLAZE DIRECT
If you are applying the glaze directly to the wall you can miss out steps 1–4 and make the brush strokes straight on to the surface. You will invariably use more glaze this way and get a more intense colour.

Rag Rolling

The principle of rag rolling is to cover the surface with a coloured glaze and then wipe it off with a rag, using a rolling motion, to give a subtle, suede-like effect. The rag produces quite a large pattern, so the technique is suitable for wide expanses such as walls and ceilings. Rag rolling can also be applied to large pieces of furniture, but a smaller rag must be used.

The secret of successful rag rolling is not to let the pattern become too uniform or regimented. You achieve this by gently changing the direction of the rolling motion as you work.

Several variations can be produced by using either a different material or a different method of patterning. Pressing the rag on to the glaze rather than rolling it will make an altogether different mark. The actual fabric also has a great bearing on the finish. Muslin will make one particular type of linear pattern, whereas a textured fabric – perhaps one with a slub weave or towelling – will make another. Instead of fabric you can use chamois leather, or paper and polythene bags. Polythene in particular makes a sharper, more detailed, mark than cloth; however it is not absorbent, so the bag must be replaced frequently to prevent it putting splodges of glaze back on to the surface as the paint builds up. Pressing bags on to the glaze is sometimes referred to as bagging, and pressing cloth is occasionally called ragging on rather than rag rolling.

Another material to use is a natural or synthetic sponge. They will give even more variation to the finish, depending on whether they are pressed or rolled on to the glaze. This last technique is called sponging off, as it removes glaze from the surface and looks quite different from the sponging technique described in Chapter 4 which transfers paint and colour on to the surface. Rag rolling is really characterised by rolling the material over the surface in all different directions to achieve a wonderful crushed velvet or creased fabric finish.

The most distinguishing marks in rag rolling will come from a dark translucent oil glaze over eggshell paint. It is also the easiest to work with, as the leading edge does not dry too quickly and the paint is not absorbed too much. If the wall is lined first, you will get a slightly more matt result that deepens the texture of the rag roll and gives it the slightly furred effect of suede. Paint alone will have more of a sheen and can be finished with a coat of polyurethane varnish to make it hard-wearing and more lustrous.

Colour combinations need to be harmonious, as rag rolling produces a busy pattern and the effect can be unpleasant if the colours seem to be fighting each other. A very sophisticated finish can be achieved by tinting ivory on ivory or white on white, using raw sienna or burnt umber in the glaze. This will be cool and interesting and can make a smaller interior look spacious and open. Darker shades of the same colour over a lighter base colour will blend well, and some stronger contrasts work if they are in the same colour scheme – for instance terracotta on pale apricot, or purple on lilac.

To put the glaze on, a roller is recommended rather than a brush. If you use a brush you will inevitably have brush marks and varying depths of colour on the wall. While this is what you want for colour washing, it is not such a suitable background for rag rolling. A much faster and easier technique is to apply the glaze with a throw-away sponge roller of the type designed for use with gloss and eggshell oil-bound paint.

If you do use a brush, it will take you a lot longer to put the glaze on. This is because the

The effect of rag rolling is an overall softness and translucence, where light shines on the glaze.

traditional way to eliminate the brush marks is to stipple them out. Time must be spent on this before you begin to work on the actual effect, otherwise brush marks will show through the rag roll. This delay puts pressure on you to work within the drying time, so you can only glaze a 1 m (3 ft) strip at a time if you are to keep the essential wet edge that makes the effect work. It often requires two people to do this well.

But by rolling the glaze on you can do an entire average-sized wall in one go, very quickly. You will still have sufficient time to rag roll it, without worrying about whether you are keeping the wet edge, as your glaze will be taken to the edges of the wall. The raw linseed oil that you add to the glaze will help to inhibit drying.

Practise first on a recess wall or other smaller area to get the hang of the rag roll technique. Then, once you have established a steady pace, you can work a larger area on your own.

How to Rag Roll

MATERIALS

- Paint tray
- Throw-away sponge roller to apply glaze
- A good quantity of the same fabric
- Base colour paint
- Brushes to apply base colour
- Glaze
- Small brush for corners and edges

PREPARATION

Cut several pieces of rag from the same cloth to the same size. Lining the wall is optional (see pp. 22 and 114). Apply two coats of eggshell paint on the surface to be colour washed. Make sure the second coat is dry, then mix the glaze to the required consistency and colour. Test it first on an area that will not be seen.

HINT

Whenever you are using glaze, it is essential to mix up enough for the whole room – do not try to do it in several batches as the resulting colours could vary considerably.

TECHNIQUE

The technique of rag rolling is designed to give a very agile, textured pattern that does not become uniform or regular. It is necessary to roll the rag in short bursts in different directions, changing the pressure slightly and frequently opening out the rag so that it does not stay in the same shape for too long. It is quite easy to get into the swing of it and keep moving over the area to be painted. If the leading edge (that is, the limit of the glaze) stays slightly wet, you will be able to add sections without creating lines or overlaps in the rag rolling.

1. Pour glaze into the paint tray and roll it on to the wall.

2. Use a brush for the corners, following the same procedure for keeping a wet edge.

3. Starting in the bottom left-hand corner, work up and out from the bottom edge. Bunch up the rag and roll it over and over under the fingertips of both hands, pressing against the surface using varying pressures. Work the rag in all different directions, covering the whole area.

4. If the wall is too large to work in one go, roller one section of it and rag roll to within 12 cm (5 in) of the leading edge. Rag roll the second strip, working out from the first strip so that the patterning continues in the same fashion. Avoid over-working a particular area as too much glaze will come off and leave a pale patch. Also avoid repairing areas: it is usually better to wipe it clean and start again.

KEEPING THE BRUSH OR CLOTH CLEAR

As soon as the brush or cloth gets too dense with glaze, replace it. You will need to do so at regular intervals. Keep opening and re-bunching the cloth to avoid making the same repetitive mark. If you are using chamois leather, soak it in white spirit first to enable you to clean it.

RAGGING

The other method is to bundle the rag into a larger wad and press it to the glaze. This is called ragging. It makes a different kind of mark and is much faster than rag rolling. However, you must still re-bunch the cloth frequently to avoid making too regular a pattern.

Dragging

Broken colour techniques lend a lustre and movement to the surface they are applied to. Dragging in particular gives a spacious effect that flat colour seems unable to achieve. It is based on the technique of wood graining, adapted to contemporary styles.

Dragging refers to the effect of painting on a transparent glaze in strong, downward strokes and then dragging it off in straight, vertical lines so that the base coat shows through. The basic effect in its simplest form is that of a woven cotton fabric. However, as with all these treatments, different combinations of tools, colours and styles of application will achieve a range of different finishes.

The glaze can be applied in layers of different colours, or it can be dragged first horizontally and then vertically. Criss-crossing in the same colour gives a gauze effect, whereas using one colour glaze in one direction and another in the opposite direction gives a woven texture. In both cases softly dragged lines that are less than straight do not disturb the overall effect. Another alternative is to apply the glaze in short strokes in all different directions, then drag it vertically. This gives a shot silk finish.

The dragging technique is at its most beautiful in a glaze over oil-bound paint that has an eggshell finish. It is also hard-wearing and gives sharp definition to the colour and texture of the dragged lines. A glaze is much easier to work with, as it stays wet for longer and makes a professional, even finish easier to achieve.

Colour combinations are the magical element of dragging. Keep white for the palest of glazes and use a base coat in a similar tone for stronger colours – too strong a contrast shows up the slightest discrepancy in the pattern and can be unpleasant to look at. Another problem arises when using two strong colours for base coat and glaze. Because the lines are so close together, the base coat cannot be visually distinguished from the glaze at a distance of more than 30–60 cm (1 2 ft). They tend to merge, and can turn muddy if they do not complement each other. Interesting results – even dramatic ones – can be achieved by combining colours that work together in two separate glazes, leaving the base coat to harmonise as a background. Experiment with colour combinations on lining paper, and stand well back to see the overall effect.

This technique requires a finely prepared, smooth surface. Unlike rag rolling and colour washing, where a regular pattern should be avoided, dragging is characteristically more uniform. The fine vertical lines draw attention to any irregularity, and sometimes the most difficult part of dragging is getting those lines straight.

It is hard to drag into corners and along edges, so this technique is usually restricted to the area below the chair rail on walls, or to panels. If the whole wall is to be covered, plan to run it to a border of some sort so that the dragged lines go from chair rail to skirting board or from picture rail to chair rail. If it is to go from skirting to ceiling, have a painted or wallpaper border over the top edge of the dragging. It gives a professional finish to a technique that invariably looks odd where it trails off.

If you apply the glaze with a brush you will have lots of little brush marks and a variety in the depth of colour on the wall. A much faster and easier technique is to apply the glaze with a throw-away sponge roller of the type designed to be used with gloss and eggshell oil-bound paint. A roller has the same advantage over a brush for dragging as it does for rag rolling (see p. 42).

These kitchen units have been dragged in a blue glaze on a pale blue base. The overall effect is cool and clean, with a touch of hand-made charm.

How to Drag

MATERIALS

- Paint tray
- Throw-away sponge roller to apply glaze
- Dragging brush in size to suit area to be covered
- Cloth of suitable material if preferred to brush
- Base colour paint
- Brushes to apply base colour
- Glaze
- Small brush for feathering out corners and edges
- Plenty of dry rags or kitchen paper to clean brushes

PREPARATION

Walls need to be well prepared for dragging as it readily shows marks. Lining is optional (see p. 114). Paint two coats of eggshell paint on the surface to be dragged. Make sure the second coat is dry, then mix the glaze to the required consistency and colour. Test it first on an area that will not be seen.

TECHNIQUE

Dragging takes a little practice to get an even pressure – particularly while ladders are being negotiated. Bear in mind that minor swerves and wobbles will not show when the finished room is restored to normal and filled with furnishings. The glaze, as for rag rolling, is best applied with a sponge roller. This saves time and allows you to work alone, covering a large area at a time with steady lines, at an even pace.

DRAGGING

1. Pour glaze into the paint tray and roll it on to the wall.

2. Use a small brush for the corners and along the edges. Feather in the marks where you have stopped and started, using an almost dry brush.

3. Starting at the left-hand side, work your way across the wall. Place the brush at the top and press the bristles against the wall. Gradually slide the brush down and away as you release the pressure with the other hand. Keep the line as straight as possible by making firm strokes, not too slowly, and keeping a strong, flexible hand to the brush.

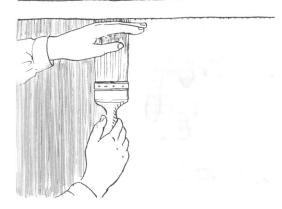

4. If the wall is too large to work in one go, roller one section of it and drag to within 12 cm (5 in) of the leading edge. Then drag the second section, working out from the first so that the lines continue in the same fashion. Avoid over-working a particular area as too much glaze will come off and leave a pale patch. Also avoid repairing areas – it is usually better to wipe it clean and start again.

KEEPING THE BRUSH CLEAR
As soon as the dragging brush gets too dense with glaze, wipe it dry on a rag. Alternatively, change cloths if that is what you are using. You will need to do this at regular intervals.

MAKING A T-SQUARE
A T-square is simply made from strips of 5 x 5 cm (2 x 2 in) timber. Nail the crossbars at each end, using a spirit level to check the right-angles. The straight edge along which you will guide the brush stands away from the wall.

HINT
The secret to straight lines is a T-square. Hang it from the picture or dado rail and run the brush down the wall, keeping the handle against the T-square. But remember too that less than straight lines create a delightful hand-done look.

Stippling, Shading and Distressing

Like dragging and rag rolling, stippling can have a number of different looks within the scope of the technique. The effect depends on the type of paint, the stippling tool and the infinite variations of colour. The size of the pattern is very small, so it is well suited to furniture and woodwork as well as to large expanses of wall. Like the effects previously described, it is created by painting on a glaze and then lifting it off the base colour. It makes an excellent base for other paint effects and for such techniques as shading and distressing.

Stippling creates a very soft finish that can range from tiny, delicate flecks of broken colour to a larger mottled pattern with more distinction to the marks. It is sometimes referred to as having an orange peel texture, although the overall finish on a large area can appear soft and cloudy or like the velvety blush on a peach skin.

Colour combinations are important, because the ground colour is not as distinct from the glaze as in rag rolling and the colours therefore merge. It is best to keep to two or three colours or shades and test them to see whether they work harmoniously together. Strong contrasts between the glaze and the base colour can also look stunning. However, before you embark on such a project it is worth comparing the types of mark made in the glaze by different tools. Sometimes the contrast is lost, or it can merge to an overall muddiness when you stand back from it.

Typically the bottom half of a wall, known as the dado, would be dragged (or papered) and only the top part stippled. It can be quite a tiring technique to apply, so it is fortunate that it can be combined so well with other paint effects.

There are invariably surprises in store from a couple of hours spent experimenting with stippling on a sheet of hardboard, painted in eggshell and hung on the wall. The usual stippling brushes, which are available in a number of sizes, create the most traditional effect. Strictly speaking, stippling is done with a brush – but it does not have to be a stippling brush. A household brush or a shoe brush for smaller areas will work too.

A roller can be used (mohair or wool, not sponge) to lift off the glaze, which makes the task much faster and easier. However, it takes some practice and the glaze must be thin or you may skid over the surface.

A wad of cloth, dabbed as you would a stippling brush, will give a softer fleck than the tiny sharp marks of a brush. These will vary according to the type of fabric used – a large weave such as sacking will produce a very different effect from a linen or muslin rag.

Experiment with a variety of tools to arrive at the pattern that works for your chosen colours and area to be painted.

A transparent oil glaze over oil-bound paint such as eggshell will give the best results and will be more forgiving to work with, as odd skid marks and lines or patches can be more easily stippled out before it dries. The glaze is applied with a throw-away sponge roller and then stippled with a brush or a wool roller.

Shading and distressing are relatively simple extensions of the stippling technique which give the subtlest of finishes to mouldings on fireplaces, covings, ceiling roses, door panels and woodwork. These are painted, glazed (using a brush to ensure that the glaze gets well into the corners), stippled and then gently wiped with a rag that takes the glaze off only the most prominent parts of the surface. This leaves the glaze colour to lie in the 'creases' or 'folds' at the base of the moulding or in the lines of the door

The strength of colour here is muted by the broken colour technique of stippling. It creates a warm effect which is less hard than solid paint might be in this instance.

frame. Shading can offset stippled and dragged walls or panels beautifully and these techniques can be used together very successfully.

Stippling everything, including walls, woodwork and doors, can, however, be a little overwhelming as all the decoration merges into an indistinct blur. Simply adding plain or distressed colour to woodwork and doors, or combining two paint effects, will give the room shape and distinction.

HINT
Carvings or mouldings that can be painted look beautiful if a medium to dark glaze is used on a light background. It is stippled and all but wiped off, leaving the moulding subtly outlined.

How to Stipple, Shade and Distress

MATERIALS

- Paint tray
- Throw-away sponge roller to apply glaze
- Stippling brush in a size to suit the area to be covered
- Cloth of suitable material if preferred to brush
- Wool roller if preferred to brush
- Base colour paint
- Brushes to apply base colour
- Glaze
- Small brush for corners and edges
- Plenty of dry rags or kitchen paper to clean brushes

PREPARATION

Walls need to be well prepared for stippling – being such a small pattern, it can show marks. Lining the wall is optional (see p. 114). Apply two coats of eggshell paint on the surface to be colour washed. Make sure the second coat is dry, then mix the glaze to the required consistency and colour, testing it first on an area that will not be seen.

TECHNIQUE

Stippling requires a firm dabbing motion. If you are using a cloth or brush, press it to the glaze and then lift it off without allowing it to slide over the glaze at all. If using a wool roller, roll it evenly over the surface and take great care to avoid skid marks. Keeping the glaze quite thin will help to prevent this. The glaze, as for rag rolling, is best applied with a sponge roller. This saves time and allows you to work alone, covering a large area at a time at an even pace. A large stippling brush is useful for bigger areas, while corners and marks can be treated by dabbing with a small dry brush to blend them in.

STIPPLING

1. Pour glaze into the paint tray and roll it on to the wall.

2. Starting at one side, work your way across the wall. Dab the cloth or stippling brush, or use the roller almost dry, working until you have a good even pattern to the stipple.

3. For the corners, brush a line of glaze down and stipple it out with a small dry brush.

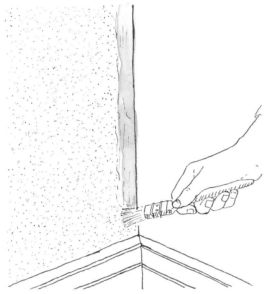

4. If the wall is too large to work in one go, roller one section of it and stipple to within 12 cm (5 in) of the leading edge. Stipple the second section working out from the first, so that the stippling continues in the same fashion. Avoid repairing large areas – it is usually better to wipe it clean and start again. But stippling is more forgiving than dragging, and once the whole wall is covered small mistakes will be lost in the overall finish.

KEEPING THE BRUSH CLEAR
As soon as the brush or cloth gets too dense with glaze, clean it on a new rag or paper towel. You will need to do this at regular intervals.

SHADING AND DISTRESSING
Paint on the glaze with a small brush, pushing it into the recesses. Use a small stippling brush to make the marks over flat or curved surfaces, stippling gently into the cracks and lines to break up the colour a little. While wet, wipe over the moulding with a clean rag so that only the prominent surface is cleaned off, leaving deeper colour in the recesses.

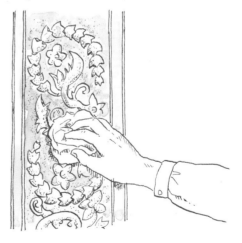

HINT
It is a good idea to paint a 60 cm (2 ft) square of hardboard when you apply the eggshell to the surface being treated. This becomes your test panel to try out colours, combinations and brush strokes before you start.

Alternative Ideas

SIMPLE BAGGING

Here is a quick and easy effect that will hide a multitude of sins. Choose your base colour and paint two coats of it in eggshell over existing wallpaper or a painted surface. Forget about any blemishes as they will add to the effect. Mix a small bottle of white spirit with a very small amount of oil-bound paint in a paint kettle until it is the colour intensity you want. Take a black plastic bin liner, scrunch it up, dip it into the 'glaze' and press and roll it on to the base colour. It is messy and haphazard, but the results are delightfully rewarding and instant – especially if you choose a good colour combination.

SPONGING OFF

This technique is very quick and easy. While it makes a similar mark to sponging (see Chapter 4), the finish is stronger and more translucent as it is a reverse method and used with an oil-bound glaze. You will not get the build-up of layered colour that you do with sponging, but even so it is a very attractive treatment. Simply roller the wall with your glaze and lift it off with a natural sponge, keeping the marks irregular. If you press and twist the sponge you will get the effect of bull's eye glass.

4
More Effects with Paint

Chapter 3 dealt with paint effects that work on the principle of adding a glaze to the wall or surface and lifting it off with different tools and techniques to create a variety of effects. This chapter explains how to produce a range of effects that involve adding paint colour to the surface.

When a glaze is being used for broken colour techniques, by nature it has a translucent finish that works over large areas. These effects, however, are usually then treated with more viscous and opaque paint colours. Less paint of a more intense mix is applied to the wall, and some of these decorations are used as borders rather than to cover a large expanse. The principle remains the same: adding colour in one form or another over a base or ground colour. Colour combinations are therefore crucial to the success of the overall effect.

Many tools are suitable for adding paint. Besides the conventional range of brushes and rollers there are numerous types of sponge and rag, each of which produces a different pattern. Beyond this there is scope for using household objects and fruit and vegetables. In fact all kinds of unusual items can be used to form attractive shapes and they can each be used in different

In this chapter:
- Sponging on
- Roller stripes
- Stamping
- Spackling
- Alternative ideas

ways – the variations are endless and limited only by your imagination.

The main techniques described in Chapters 3 and 4 are frequently combined. The ones detailed in this chapter can be used as a finishing touch to a background of stippling or colour wash. Everything depends on the nature of the room and the strength of colour in the background. A pastel colour wash, for example, can be enhanced by a border of stamping, while stippling is a very effective ground for some types of sponging. There are not really any hard-and-fast rules about what will or will not work. It really is a question of trying out the different effects and seeing how they go together. Test them by hanging samples on a wall so that you can then stand back and get an idea of the overall effect alongside your existing colour scheme and furnishings.

Sponging On

This bright, textured effect is quickly and easily achieved. You can use several paint types and vary the number of colours, or layers, of sponging. It can, for instance, be treated as the techniques in Chapter 3, where a glaze is applied to the wall and lifted off with a natural sponge, leaving distinctive marks on the wall. This is sometimes referred to as sponging off.

But this chapter, as already explained, deals with different ways of applying paint on to the surface, and this technique is often called sponging on. A marine sponge is still used; however, with this method it is dipped into the colour and pressed to the wall in order to leave its characteristic mark. The following pages explain how to use an unusual combination of paint types that is easy to work and extremely effective, as it gives the finished treatment a three-dimensional look. It also has a subtle lustre similar to that of a glaze, even though the paint is all water-based.

It is often recommended to sponge on with oil-based paint and actually apply the glaze to the wall as if it was paint. This is certainly possible, and can look lovely when layers of translucent colour are built up. However, the sponge gets very sticky and it is not the easiest of methods. Using emulsion paint makes the actual sponging very manageable, as the colour is diluted with water and so it is easier to control the saturation of the sponge. Ordinary emulsion, however, tends to absorb the colours and produce a flat-looking finish. Fortunately this problem is completely overcome if you use a vinyl silk emulsion. Two coats of this as a background colour make an excellent base to work on and give a gentle sheen to the finished treatment. It is also kind to beginners, as mistakes can be wiped off within the drying time.

Sponging on is an invitation to use bright, dancing colours that suit its light-hearted style. These work best if they are well coordinated. Too strong a combination will produce a busy, dramatic effect that could be quite difficult to live with. The marks are not as small and speckled as in stippling and the bigger, mottled pattern of the sponge is best supported by subtle, matching tones from at least two of the three colours used.

This method of sponging on is best used on large surfaces, such as walls, that will take water-based paint. Smaller areas, such as furniture, are better treated to an oil-based glaze on eggshell paint using a very small sponge, so that the marks are not too big for the item they are decorating.

The effect is created by first painting the entire surface in the base colour in vinyl silk. The next layer of colour consists of matt emulsion paint mixed half-and-half with water. This is sponged on all over the base, with the sponge marks close enough to touch and often overlap, making a cloudy effect that the base shines through. The last – and usually the strongest – colour is made up of water tinted with universal stainer or artist's acrylic paint. This is then applied quite sparsely over the first layer with a smaller sponge, giving a marvellous depth to the overall finish. With practice and confidence yet another colour can be sparsely used.

Decide on your colour scheme and choose two similar shades, or closely coordinated colours, for the base and first layer of sponging. For pastel colouring avoid a stark white base – use off-white, cream or another pale colour instead. This works well if the first layer of sponging is done in a stronger shade of the same colour group. The contrast colour is left to the

Sponging on is done in layers of colour on a background that blends with it. Here yellow, white and peach have been sponged on to a rough-textured salmon-coloured wall. The combined effect is that of pale terracotta.

end, where its intensity is diluted by the thin consistency of the mixture. If you prefer darker colours, then still use matching shades of, say, tans or greens for the base and first layer, keeping a brighter contrast or lighter highlight for the sparsely sponged top layer. White can look lovely as the first layer of sponging over a cream or pastel base, enriched with a top layer in a much darker colour.

As with all these techniques, it is very important to make a test panel. When you paint the two coats of vinyl silk on the wall, do one or two test panels at the same time (a 45 cm/18in square of hardboard is perfect). It is always worth playing with different colour combinations, as you will invariably be surprised at the range and variety of effects you can achieve with this technique.

How to Sponge On

MATERIALS

- Vinyl silk emulsion in base colour
- Roller and tray for emulsion
- Small brush for corners and cutting in
- Matt emulsion for first layer of sponging (tint white or buy a match pot)
- Marine sponges – at least one for each colour and small pieces for corners
- Roll of kitchen paper
- Artist's acrylic paint or universal stainers for second and third colours
- Water
- Dish or saucer

HINT
Prepare one or two sample boards at the same time by painting them in two coats of vinyl silk when you paint the wall.

PREPARATION

The wall surface should be smooth, as the effect of light on this technique will show up blemishes and bumps. Consider lining a badly marked or pitted wall before painting. Paint the wall or surface to be sponged with two coats of vinyl silk emulsion. Make sure the paint is completely dry before sponging.

TECHNIQUE

Sponging involves a gentle dabbing action: press the sponge to the wall and lift it straight off to exploit the lovely markings that the holes in a natural sponge can leave. For the first layer of sponging, the paint is thinned to the texture of cream. Make sure that you move the sponge around in your hand and apply the marks in all different directions. The natural tendency is to form orderly lines, and any regularity of pattern spoils the spontaneity of the effect.

The second layer of sponging is done with tinted water, so it is very fluid. Have plenty of kitchen paper to hand and immerse the sponge into the cup of colour, gently squeezing it out without wringing it dry. Press it on to the kitchen paper to absorb the excess before daubing the sponge on to the wall. Leave the corners and edges initially, because if a large sponge is pressed to one side of a corner it will bruise the other side. When the rest of the sponging is dry, take a small piece of sponge and just do the wall either side of the corner and along skirtings, doorways and similar areas. You can wipe off any marks on woodwork with a damp cloth before it dries.

1. Mix the first layer of sponge colour in the dish or saucer, using half emulsion paint and half water. Add acrylic colour as necessary until you have achieved the colour you require, and mix well.

2. Wet the sponge and squeeze it out completely to prime it. Dip it in the paint mixture and dab off any excess on kitchen paper. It should not be dripping.

3. Press the sponge to the wall, making the marks close together or even overlapping them. Make sure you work haphazardly, and keep moving the sponge in your hand to stop it 'printing' the same marks in too regular a fashion. Let this coat dry.

4. Mix the water in the cup with acrylic colour or universal stainer until you have the density of colour you require. Immerse a small natural sponge in the mixture and squeeze it out, but not too much. Press the sponge on to kitchen paper until it makes fine marks that do not run.

5. Press the top colour to the wall in sparse, irregularly placed dabs that leave the first layer of sponging clearly visible. Where the top colour overlaps the edges of the sponged circles on the first layer, a soft three-dimensional effect is created.

Roller Stripes

Rollers are wonderful tools that cover an area quickly and easily and have transformed the time it takes to paint large expanses of wall and ceiling. They are conventionally used for making a wide, even mark that when correctly applied leaves a solid, flat finish (see p. 26).

However, a roller does not have to be limited to solid areas. There are different types of rollers which are designed to be used with the various paints available.

Even then the roller itself can be made more versatile – it can be bound so as to put all kinds of different lines and patterns on to the surfaces. These can be very successfully used as broken colour techniques, such as those described in Chapter 3. If you paint on a glaze and use a bound roller to lift it off you can achieve all kinds of results, depending on the cloth, string or other material used to bind it.

One method involves simply tying a tight string around the middle of a sponge roller, so that it can paint two stripes with every stroke – omitting a band of colour down the middle. The width and number of the stripes can be varied according to the number of times you bind the roller. Another effect is created with rough string, or twine with a hairy texture. This can be wrapped around the roller sponge firmly – but not tightly enough to draw it in very far. If the twine remains in contact with the wall it will fleck the work slightly as you go. The twine needs to be changed regularly before it gets saturated with glaze. You can use torn strips of fabric in exactly the same way.

A small area such as a toy box or a cupboard door can be jazzed up using a very small roller (such as those found in toyshops) and rolling first vertically and then horizontally to create checks. If the paint is thin, or just a coloured glaze, at the place where the stripes cross you will get a deeper colour from the two layers. Entire walls can be done this way – particularly with pale colours – if the boldness of the pattern suits the room. The colours can be changed with the direction – a yellow ground with an ochre horizontal stripe and a sienna or mid-green vertical stripe creates a warm, vibrant combination. In a thin glaze, it can almost look as if the walls are wrapped in light blankets.

There is a great deal of scope for density of paint, colour combinations and width, number and direction of the stripes. They do not have to cover the whole wall, particularly if you are using strong colours. Stripes can be taken from the skirting board to the chair rail, meeting a horizontal band of colour or a border. Another, softer, paint effect can be used on the top part of the wall, or it can be left plain in one of the stripe colours. This is preferable if the walls are to have a number of pictures on them. Stencilling (see Chapter 5) can also be added to roller stripes.

These techniques will give a different effect again when you apply paint, rather than glaze, to the wall. Instead of a translucent finish that shows wisps of string and subtle layers of colour, you will get a more definite mark or stripe. It is the simplicity of these informally drawn strips of colour that makes them so delightful in plain paint.

Roller stripes can be softly blended and overlapped, or a gap can be allowed in between the lines.
Here the radiator has been treated as part of the wall, which often works well with broken colour techniques.

How to Do Roller Stripes

MATERIALS

- One roller per colour being used
- Various rollers for different-width stripes if preferred
- One paint tray per colour being used
- Base colour paint
- Paint or glaze for making stripes
- Strong elastic band
- Lining paper to test glaze colour
- Plumbline
- HB pencil

Binding a roller gives an unusual finish similar to rag rolling.

PREPARATION

Walls need to be well prepared before you embark on this technique, and will benefit from being lined (see p. 114). Paint one or two coats of eggshell paint in the base colour. Make sure the second coat is dry before you proceed. Lay out some strips of lining paper on a small table, to enable you to remove excess paint from the roller as you work. Bind the roller tightly in the middle with the elastic band to form two stripes.

TECHNIQUE

Roller stripes are achieved by holding the roller with a steady hand and working in one direction with a smooth downward or horizontal stroke. One of the reasons for covering only smaller areas by this method is that on large expanses the roller can need replenishing mid-stripe. However this may be turned into part of the design, or it can be disguised if the roller is primed first. Load it with paint and try it out on lining paper first so that the whole roller is evenly saturated. If the stripe is long, roll until the intensity of the paint begins to fade. Reload the roller, remove any excess on your scraps of lining paper, then begin again over the stripe so that there is a good overlap where the colour began to fade. Do not attempt to make stop and start lines meet – overlap them. If the paint has a wet leading edge it should merge well and leave no obvious lines.

HINT
It is a good idea to hang a sheet of lining paper up on the wall to test colours, combinations and brush strokes before you start.

---

1. Mark up the wall using a plumbline so that you know where each stripe is to start, leaving a gap the width of the blank between the stripes, or a longer one if you prefer. Make the marker lines very lightly in pencil.

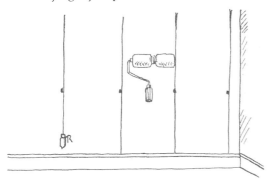

2. Paint a vertical stripe with the roller, using your lines as a guide. Do not worry if the line is not perfectly straight – it adds to the appeal of this hand-made 'wallpaper'.

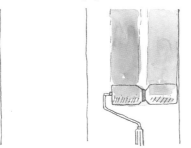

3. For horizontal lines repeat steps 1 and 2, using a spirit level to make the markers. Make sure the first stripes are completely dry, or the roller will lift off the glaze underneath as you go. It is also possible to work by eye, giving an even more hand-finished look.

4. You can vary the pattern by making the gaps different widths and using a variety of roller sizes, binding them in different places. Alternatively, a plaid effect can look stunning all in the same colour, using a narrow roller for a smaller-width stripe.

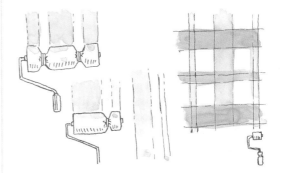

5. Different colours can be used on every other stripe, or on the cross lines. As the glaze forms a double coat where the stripes cross, you will get a deeper intensity of colour there – much like a woven fabric. Choose colours carefully so that they do not go muddy.

Stamping

It takes a certain amount of confidence to make pictures with paint in a freehand style. Often it is safer to go the stencilling route, where the actual motif is prepared and accurately repeats (see Chapter 5). However, a great deal of pleasure can be had with potato cuts and other means of stamping a simple shape and repeating the design all around a room. It is the sheer playfulness of the shapes that gives them their character.

In its simplest form stamping is like the earliest print technique of taking a block with a shape on it, dipping it in colour (ink) and pressing it to the paper. The technique is really that straightforward. Although printing evolved to become very elaborate, with the block itself becoming ever more finely detailed, stamping is usually characterised by a cruder shape that has a rough definition and boldness to it. Many different pieces of equipment and objects can be used to make the stamp: technically, anything that can be readily handled and will pick up paint and make a satisfactory mark with it.

Mechanical printing, using manufactured objects, can be used to simulate wallpaper and cover a whole wall with a repeating design. Outlines in squares or rounds can be picked up from small, sturdy cardboard boxes – or you can make your own shapes from corrugated card. Corks are available in a variety of sizes for in-between marks, or else use nails and nuts and bolts from the toolbox. You can also create blocks by attaching a handle to the back of a small rectangle of wood about 7.5 x 15 cm (3 x 6 in) and sticking various things to it to 'block print' with. Synthetic sponge, polystyrene, string and cord can all be stuck on to make a variety of patterns for printing. Indeed, the familiar flat washing-up sponges are easy to draw on and cut

out – choose shapes by photocopying designs in books and tracing them on to the sponge.

Vegetables are another wonderful source of stamps, taking you back perhaps to your early days at school. Sprouts and cabbages cut in half will make delightful random circular shapes, while different-sized potatoes, carrots and parsnips are very easy to handle. Some vegetables get 'tired' quite quickly, so you need a good stock of them. Play about on lining paper until you have a simple and attractive range of motifs and colour combinations.

The type of paint used for stamping can vary and need not be applied to a background of plain colour. Colour washing and stippling make good bases, as will a glaze that has been simply rolled on. It can be lifted off with a sponge or cloth to create a simple textured finish – either will make an interesting background for stamping. Once the base glaze is dry you can apply the stamped designs using more coloured glazes. This will give you a very versatile range of colours and lend a slight translucency to the marks. This is ideal for stamping that is intended to cover the whole wall, like a hand-made wallpaper, as the motif is less likely to become overpowering.

For shapes that require more depth or intensity of colour – such as those that will form a simple border around the room – you can apply children's PVA paint or white emulsion mixed with gouache. Silk finish emulsion will give a slight shine to the result, and all these water-based paints can be applied directly to an emulsion base. Because of the simplicity of the method and the design style, the paint consistency is one of preference rather than necessity. A block that is to cover the whole wall will produce a gentler effect on the eye – and be

This simple square has been stamped in a border pattern all around the kitchen.
The marks have a hand-made feel to them and make the atmosphere cosy and informal.

easier to work with – if you use emulsion paint watered down to the consistency of milk. Use a sponge, as it will absorb the excess water. With non-absorbent blocking tools and small, strong designs the paint can be applied undiluted, which will leave thick textured marks.

There is so much scope and possibility that after a morning spent playing about on lining paper you may well be short of walls for all the different designs you have come up with. Keep the choice for walls and floors simple – it often works best – and frame some of the results of your experimenting on lining paper as a finishing touch to the room!

How to Stamp

MATERIALS

- Water-based paints made up of coloured emulsion, *or*
- PVA paints that are bright and thick in texture
- Roller
- Sheet of glass
- Knife or scissors for cutting shapes
- Block
- Household washing-up sponge
- PVA glue
- Block of wood 18 x 10 cm (7 x 4 in)
- Small door handle
- Rags and kitchen towels
- Household paintbrush
- Paper
- Black felt-tip pen

PREPARATION

Stamping can be used as a border at picture rail height or at dado rail height. It can also be used in a regular pattern all over the wall like a mock wallpaper. In either case it has a naturally hand-produced feel that does not demand immaculately prepared walls, and even looks good on rough plaster if it is compatible with the style of the room. You can paint the wall in two coats of a background colour in matt or silk emulsion, depending on whether or not you want the effect to have a sheen to it. You can also apply another paint technique, as stamping looks well over colour washed or stippled walls.

Cut out a simple shape in paper and transfer it to the household sponge in black felt pen. Then fix the door handle on to the back of the block of wood.

TECHNIQUE

Dip the object you are using to make the mark into the paint and literally 'stamp' with it over the area being decorated. To cover the object in the paint, first roll some out on to a sheet of glass and then press the object on to it. This helps to prevent excess blobs of paint taking different shapes or running. Alternatively, if you are using a block you can apply paint to the motif with a brush or roller. Use a dabbing motion that presses the motif to the wall repeatedly. Water-based paints tend to work best for this technique: they are better absorbed, particularly if you are using vegetables.

WORKING WITH A BLOCK

1. Cut out the design and stick it to the underside of the block of wood using the PVA glue.

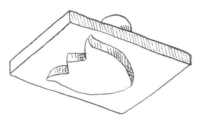

2. Either roll the paint on to a piece of glass and press the block on to it, or roll the paint straight on to the sponge side of the block.

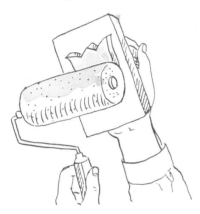

3. Using the block, press the design over the wall, making a simple print. You can repeat this in a different colour, or add another shape to the design.

WORKING WITH A SPONGE ALONE

Alternatively you can cut the shape out from a thick car sponge with a knife. Draw the design on the sponge and cut away the surplus to a depth of about 2.5 cm (1 in). The motif is then standing proud and the whole sponge becomes the block.

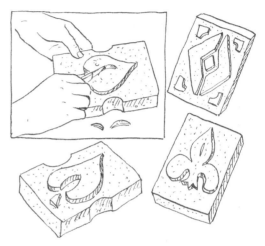

STAMPS FROM VEGETABLES

Vegetables such as sprouts or small cabbages can be cut in half and used, and potatoes can have lovely simple shapes cut out of them. Replace them as you work if they get soft or too heavily covered in paint.

Spackling

This technique, which is sometimes referred to as colour splashing or spattering, is one which can work well over large areas such as floors and walls. It is great fun – and very messy! The effect can be created in many different ways and, although you have less control than with other paint finishes, it is this very element of unpredictability that makes the result so delightful.

The basic technique is to take a lightly loaded, short paintbrush and strike it against the straight edge of a piece of wood or another brush handle, spattering the paint in random spots across the surface. A stencil brush is ideal. The spackles can be built up in layers of one or more colours, and their density can be varied depending on whether you use paint or glaze.

The further away you stand, the bigger the mark. To cover the whole room evenly you have to strike the brush repeatedly against the same object, at the same distance from the surface, using the same pressure and consistency of paint. A distance of 30 cm (1 ft) and paint or glaze the consistency of milk makes a good starting point. Like all these techniques, it is worth practising. You will be surprised at how much scope there is for varying the size of the spot and the length of the spray, and creating different finishes with different colours. Paint that is very thin will run after it is spattered, whereas thick paint will make splodges – both of which work beautifully if they are the effect you want to create, but otherwise spoil the finish entirely.

Whatever refinement of spackling you finally choose, always carefully mask off the surrounding areas before you start. The sprays of paint invariably splatter further around the target than you imagine, so aim to spackle furniture outside if possible. On walls, particularly if only one section is to be treated with flecks, you will need to cover the other sections with a light plastic dust sheet attached with masking tape.

Colour is very much the key to this paint effect, and it generally works best in strong and daring contrasts. Very pale spackling on a light background tends to get lost or look as if you were trying to achieve a different technique which failed. Bright contrasts and primary colours work very well – play with red, blue and green on a sunny yellow, or pick a selection of fruit colours such as lime, tangerine or raspberry on white. Dark, strong colours work well together on a small expanse, such as furniture. Try dark reds and greens together, with a sparing spray of black and gold before you varnish. Keep the application of each glaze colour quite sparse, so that the build-up of two, three or four colours does not look overcrowded. Have fun practising first – you will quickly acquire a steady control over the specks.

In its simplest form spackling can be done with any paint type. However, the methods used in Chapter 3 for mixing glazes – applied to eggshell painted walls – will give you lovely bright results that have a texture and depth to them. These materials also allow you to change your mind – if you decide you dislike what you have done, you can simply wipe off the glaze before it has dried and start again.

The technique of spackling can be developed into the more difficult, but very rewarding, effect of porphyry – a beautiful type of granite. It contains wonderful colours including violet, green, brown and deep red, with flecks in pink or maroon, cream and black. Start by sponging in the base colour, such as red, and then spackle the surface first in a tinted pale pink glaze, then in a very dark maroon glaze. A final spackling of

This blue stool has been spackled with navy blue, yellow and white to coordinate with the white woodwork, yellow walls and blue rug.

black, sparingly applied, and one or two coats of gloss varnish give an outstanding effect.

For a different effect again, a rich bright lustre and sparkling texture will be achieved by spackling gold paint on to a wall that you have already painted. Very little is required, but, especially if it is subsequently varnished with gloss or a mid-sheen varnish, it will give you exciting results. Rich turquoises and gold, or deep reds with a gold splash over them, have a naturally opulent finish that makes a bold decorative statement in a room.

How to Spackle

MATERIALS

- Base colour in eggshell or emulsion
- Glazes in the various colours (with eggshell), *or*
- Water mixed with acrylic or universal stainers (with emulsion)
- Stencilling brush per colour
- Stick of wood with a straight edge
- Masking tape and polythene to mask off areas not to be spackled
- Lining paper to experiment

HINT

Spackling often benefits from varnishing after it has dried. Furniture in particular should be varnished to make the effect harder-wearing. Either gloss or mid-sheen may be used, and can be built up in layers for a lacquered effect. It is essential to work in a dust-free area because each layer must be perfectly finished for the lustre to achieve the right depth.

PREPARATION

Mask off any areas you do not wish to flick paint on to. Give your work a wide berth and expect to get well covered yourself. Spackling can be done using various tinted glazes, spackled on in layers, over an eggshell wall. This will give a translucent effect. Alternatively use water-based paints, keeping a vinyl silk base and matt or vinyl silk colour in bright contrast for the actual spackles. The surface of the wall need not be immaculate for this technique, especially if you intend to use several layers of colourful flecks spattered everywhere. Paint two coats of base, whichever medium you choose.

TECHNIQUE

Spackling, although it looks very simple, benefits hugely from practice. Mad flicks at the walls with a huge, laden brush can work, but the room will need to be quite large for this effect to be visually successful. At the other end of the scale, a delicate spray from flicking a toothbrush loaded with paint can look beautiful on a small side table even though it would be far too time consuming to consider for a whole wall.

Between the two is the measured spackling that can be achieved with a stencilling brush and a stick of wood; with some practice, this can be reasonably well controlled. Load the bristles of the brush, not too heavily, and hold the wood 15–22 cm (6–10 in) from the wall, hitting it sharply with the brush handle. The paint should be the consistency of milk, so that it sprays and sticks without running.

FOR WALLS AND LARGER AREAS

1. Load the tip of the brush with paint in the first colour and hold the stick of wood 15–22 cm (6–10 in) away. Bring the brush handle sharply down on to the stick, so that paint sprays over the wall.

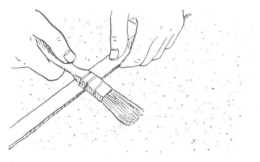

2. Repeat, making sparsely spread out flicks of paint across the wall in the first colour.

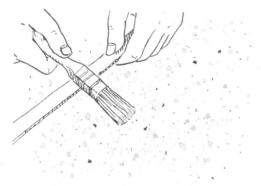

3. Using the second colour, repeat steps 1 and 2. Try standing a little further back – or a little nearer – to vary the size of the speckles. Build up two, three or four layers of coloured speckles – depending on how dense you want the finished effect to be.

FOR FURNITURE AND SMALLER AREAS

Use oil-based paint as a base. Carefully mask off any areas you do not wish to spackle. Use a small paintbrush or toothbrush full of paint and flick it on with a knife or your finger, spraying the bristles. Practise first on lining paper – once you get the hang of it, it is possible to control the marks quite well.

Alternative Ideas

MIX AND MATCH

Mixing the broken colour techniques, yet keeping to one colour, can create a beautiful effect without being monotonous. Kitchens are an excellent opportunity to try this treatment as they invariably contain a lot of different surfaces that can be exploited. Choose a base colour in a similar tone to the glaze but lighter. Try dragging the cupboards and woodwork to match, with door frames, window frames, skirting boards and cupboard trimmings slightly distressed. Then colour wash or rag roll the walls in the same colours. Finish with tiles and soft furnishings in the same background colour, perhaps picking out a complementary shade to match the flooring in the odd tile and in the fabric.

BROKEN COLOUR ADDED ON

Broken colour techniques such as colour washing can be added on to the base colour using emulsion paints instead of oil-bound glazes. They don't have the translucence of colour that comes from lifting the glaze off with a brush or other material; however, they work just as well in the right setting and can give a more subtle, matt finish. Use very diluted colour, first brushing it on to lining paper to make sure the brush, or cloth, is not saturated and will not drip. This will allow the base colour to show through (see p. 31 for quantities). The technique is equally successful when applied to furniture. Since smaller areas are usually involved, they can take a greater contrast between the base colour and the wash.

5
Stencilling

This exciting, rewarding technique can be used in a huge variety of ways and numerous decorative effects can be created. This chapter provides information on the basic techniques, the range of materials and the various methods of applying a selection of them.

One of the things that makes stencilling exciting is the immediacy and high quality of the results and the ease with which a complete beginner can achieve them. The versatility lies in the sheer range of designs and permutations and the number of different kinds of surface to which the technique can be applied. Walls, ceilings, floors, fabrics, soft furnishings, tables, chairs, shelves, cupboard fronts, tiles, china, windows and mirrors can all be treated to stencilling in the appropriate paint.

The real trick is deciding on the design and where to use it – and then balancing it with the colour and style of the room. You must also consider the optimum size of the stencilled pattern and the repeats. A border placed high on a wall will be lost if it is too small or too sparsely placed, whereas a door panel at eye level will provide the perfect frame for a small, intricate design that is only repeated once or twice. If you

In this chapter:
- Making your own stencils
- Different materials for different stencilling surfaces
- Measuring up stencils as borders and papers
- Stencils for furniture and fun
- Alternative ideas

are covering a large area of wall by making a mock wallpaper, then a large design that naturally fits together will be more successful, and easier to do, than a very small, asymmetrical one with close repeats.

Spend some time beforehand trying out designs and colour combinations on lining paper. Then attach them to the wall or furniture and stand back to get a good idea of how they would look. You will soon see if a border motif needs to be spaced out or closed up a little more, or if a design is too big or small for the intended surface. Experimenting like this enables you to select the method and materials best suited to the effect you want to create.

Making Your Own Stencils

Stencils are easily obtainable from specialist shops, craft shops, DIY stores, department stores and even by mail order. There is a fantastic variety of designs on offer, together with suggestions on ways to use them. If you have a room you would like to decorate with stencils, enjoy a few shopping trips looking at what can be bought and generally gathering information and ideas.

You can be cautious with stencilling, picking out a favourite design and placing a few repeats around the wall; this may well be all that a carefully planned room needs to finish it off. However, some time spent in a specialist shop or looking through books and magazines might inspire you to mix and match stencils for bright and bold combinations. People are often at their most relaxed and unselfconscious when decorating a small child's room. Stencilling can really come into its own in an informal atmosphere such as this; you can cover the walls with crowds of animals or teddy bears and clowns – or all sorts of other characters and shapes. It can turn you into an artist, and the child's room into a feast of decorative treatments.

If you feel adventurous – or you cannot find the kind of design you want – it is quite straightforward to make your own stencils. The best materials are either oiled manila paper that

you cut with a sharp craft knife, or acetate film that can be cut either with a knife or with a heat pen. Both materials are available from art suppliers and craft shops, and are all to be found in specialist stencil suppliers. Acetate, being transparent, is easier for transferring designs, as the motif can be traced directly on to it and cut out. However, manila paper is sometimes stronger. Your choice here will depend on how many repeats you intend to make and whether you are spraying or brushing on the paint. It is relatively easy to reproduce a stencil and cut out another one if you are doing an extensive area (see p. 76).

When you have spent some time looking for inspiration for your own designs from museums and books and magazines you will eventually arrive at a pattern or motif that you like. You then have to make sure it will work well in practical terms, with 'bridges' between the shapes where the stencil itself remains intact. You then transfer the design to the paper or acetate and cut it out with a craft knife or heat pen, leaving the edges of the holes to become the outlines of the shapes to be painted on to the wall or furniture. The bridges hold the design together both aesthetically and literally: these small uncut areas give the stencil strength. Too many large holes with lots of thin bridges will

This box has been very simply stencilled in one colour, with a border wiped on with a cloth dipped in paint and rubbed off around the edges.

make the stencil vulnerable to tearing when you lift it off to repeat it. Stencils that work well have spaces between the shapes as an integral part of the design, forming naturally sturdy bridges wherever possible. Although it is quite easy to mend stencils, it is best to make them inherently strong to start with by balancing the holes and spaces well.

Lining up the actual stencil and masking it on the wall are important elements in the process. The way to mask depends on whether you are spraying the paint or brushing it on. For spraying, the easiest method is to take a large sheet of strong cartridge paper and make a window in the middle, taping the stencil to it with masking tape so that the stencil is in the window, and leaving a wide surround of cartridge paper to protect the wall.

How to Make Your Own Stencils

MATERIALS

- Pencil
- Tracing paper
- Coloured crayons or chalks for experimenting
- Scissors
- Stencil craft paper (oiled manila board) or acetate
- Good craft knife or heat pen
- Cutting board or sheet of new hardboard or glass (with rounded edges)

HINT

Trace the outline of your stencil design and photocopy it several times. Before you start, cut out the shapes very roughly and stick them on to your chosen surface with Blue-tak or any easily removable adhesive. This will give you a sense of the spacing and effectiveness of the stencil. You can even colour your test pieces in chalk or crayon to help you achieve the right colour scheme.

PREPARATION

Find the design you like, or combination of designs, and work out a simple drawing that will be suitable as a stencil, relating the size of the motif to your purpose. Have a clean dry area to work on and enough space to move the cutting board in all directions. To try the design, copy or photocopy several on to some scrap paper and colour them in your chosen paint tone or with similar-coloured chalks or crayons.

TECHNIQUE

Cutting out your own stencils, particularly with a craft knife, is fiddly and needs patience as much as skill. Always work on a cutting board or a piece of previously unused hardboard. Attach the paper firmly to the board with masking tape all the way along the edges. Have space to work in so that when you are cutting curves you can turn the whole board, rather than trying to turn the knife. A heat pen can be easier but it only works on acetate: follow the manufacturer's instructions.

REPRODUCING A STENCIL QUICKLY

If you plan to use a stencil many times and need a copy of it, this is the best way to reproduce it. Lay the stencil over a sheet of manila card. Attach it firmly at the edges, making sure it lies completely flat. Spray the stencil just as if you were doing it on the wall, covering it densely. This will reproduce a replica of it on the bottom sheet. Remove the original, then cut out the design from the bottom sheet to form your second stencil.

CUTTING OUT A STENCIL

1. Roughly cut out the whole shapes and try them to adjust positioning.

2. Work out your final stencil design and go over it in clear black so you have a strong outline to work from.

3. Trace the design carefully on to the tracing paper with a soft pencil and copy it on to the craft paper or acetate film.

4. Cut out the shapes carefully with a craft knife, making sure the edges and corners are as neatly and cleanly cut as possible. Turn the board, not the knife, as you work.

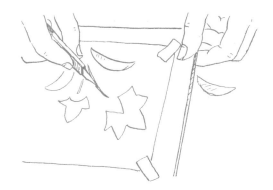

MAKING A MASK

If you intend to use spray paint for the stencil, make a mask with some lining paper. If it is a large design, use thin card instead.

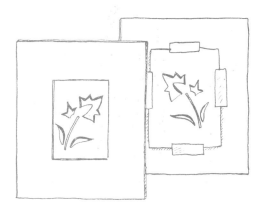

REPAIRING A STENCIL

To mend a damaged stencil, stick a piece of masking tape over the tear on both the back and front of the stencil. Then recut the stencil through the masking tape.

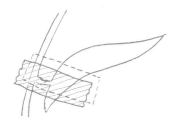

Different Materials for Stencilling Different Surfaces

Stencils can be painted on to wood, glass and fabric as well as tiles and bricks or concrete. Given the right drawing materials they can be made to go almost anywhere, inside or outside the home. Once you have created or bought your stencil design, you must select the appropriate material for the surface you wish to decorate. This will depend to some extent on the finish you want to create. Below are details of some of the different methods, together with their advantages and disadvantages, to help you decide.

SPRAY PAINTS

Using a stencilling brush can be quite tiring, especially if you are working above shoulder height. This may be acceptable for a small or sparse design, but larger stencils or those requiring many repetitions are much easier to apply with spray paint. Another advantage is the extensive range of colours and metallic finishes available in spray paints, which provides wide scope for different effects as well as being suitable for a good range of surfaces. Since they are enamels, sprays can be used on ceramic, glass and metal surfaces as well as the more conventional wood, walls and floors. Spraying also creates a distinctive effect: your stencils will have a softness similar to the results produced by air brushing, and can be built up very gently to present a lovely shaded three-dimensional appearance.

It is very important to experiment with spraying before you start. With practice you can control the finish to a surprisingly fine degree; however, there are some pitfalls that you need to learn to deal with. If you stand too close the paint will run; if you spray too short and sharp a jet you will get uneven blobs of colour; if you stand too far away you can end up spraying everything but the stencil. Set up a board or strips of lining paper on a wall to practise on. It takes a short while and a little paint, but once you have a smooth even spray working easily across the stencil, you can build it up in layers and play with the effects of layering different colours. For large areas, have at least two cans of colour available and some spare nozzles, as they do clog up occasionally.

ESSENTIAL PRECAUTIONS TO TAKE WHEN USING SPRAY PAINTS

- Mask the stencil well (see p. 77)
- Mask surrounding areas, furniture and yourself
- Wear a face mask so you avoid breathing the fumes
- Make sure you are in a room with good ventilation and fresh air circulating. Stencil furniture outside on a still day if possible
- Follow the manufacturer's instructions for use and care of spray paint, as well as cleaning
- Follow the manufacturer's warnings when using aerosols, and keep away from babies, children and pets

BRUSHABLE PAINTS AND CRAYONS

Theoretically you can use most types of paint for stencilling, and some experimenting on lining

This floor stencil has been produced in spray paint. There are different paints available for all surfaces, such as textile paint for fabrics and ceramic paint for tiles and glass.

paper or a trial area will soon reveal their properties and suitability. For tiles and glass use ceramic paints, and for fabric use paint that is specifically made for use on material. Water-based paint is fine on a lined wall or on emulsion paint. Otherwise the stencil supply shops have a wonderful range of colours in liquid and crayon form. In any case, you need very little paint for stencilling. The secret is to apply it with an almost dry stencil brush. The paint mixes easily and so, using a brush for each colour, it can be built up in layers or merged where colours overlap to give shaded effects and a three-dimensional quality. If you gently blend primary colours (see the colour wheel on p.7), you will get a soft secondary colour where they overlap.

ALTERNATIVES TO BRUSHES

For applying the paint it is also worth experimenting with other tools than an aerosol and a stencilling brush. Natural and synthetic sponges each give completely different effects with the same stencil, and so will a roller. Again, it takes some practice to mix the paint to the right consistency so that it can be built up softly and does not run behind the stencil.

With all these tools applying paint is faster than with a stencil brush. However, they do not give the same delicacy of result, so they suit some stencil designs more than others. Keep to the minimum amount of paint at a time, or else use a glaze to give a more translucent, gentle depth of colour.

How to Apply Stencils

MATERIALS

- Stencil(s)
- Chalk or chinagraph pencil
- Masking tape or spray mount (not permanent type)
- Suitable masking (lining paper)
- Lining paper to experiment on
- Paint, aerosols, glaze or other suitable stencilling material
- Cleaning solution and cloths for preparation
- Old tiles or glass or dishes for the palette and working the paint
- Plenty of kitchen paper
- Brushes, preferably one for each colour you intend to use
- Sponges or rollers for each paint colour
- Spare nozzles for aerosols if used
- Masking tape and polythene dust sheets for masking surrounding areas
- Rags and suitable cleaning materials

HINT

Spray mount, available from stencil suppliers and art materials shops, can be used sparingly on the backs of stencils. It stays tacky for several applications.

PREPARATION

Make sure the surface is clean and dry, using the recommended cleaning solution for the type of paint you are using. Otherwise use sugar soap and remove any residue. If the stencil is to be applied over a paint effect, make sure the paint is completely dry. Measure up or plan the area you are going to stencil, using chalk or a chinagraph pencil to mark the positions of the stencil design. Mask the stencil suitably and place in position with masking tape, or else spray lightly with spray mount and stick in place.

TECHNIQUE

Sprayed stencilling needs a steady, even spray of paint across the stencil. Start the spray over the mask to one side of the motif and continue across it beyond the opposite edge, so that the stencil itself benefits from the middle part of the spraying motion. Work in light layers.

If you are using a brush, again with very little paint at a time, use a dabbing motion as if you were dotting the paint on the edge of the stencil and work into the middle of the design. Sponges can also be dabbed, but ensure that they are nearly dry or the paint will run. A roller, again used almost dry, is simply rolled over the stencil. Little sponge rollers sold for craft work will do very well. Whatever you use, have plenty of kitchen paper to hand and apply the paint to the paper before you apply it to the stencil. This will ensure that your brush, sponge or other tool will be used almost dry.

If using a stencil crayon, work it into a circle on a tile to create a 'squirl' of colour; alternatively you can use the edge of the stencil as a palette. Dip the brush or sponge into the crayon colour and apply it straight to the stencil – there is no need to wipe off any surplus on kitchen paper in this instance.

USING A BRUSH

1. Place a small amount of each colour on to your palette or on to dishes or tiles. Dip the brush into the paint, dabbing it off until it is nearly dry, and finally dabbing it on some kitchen paper.

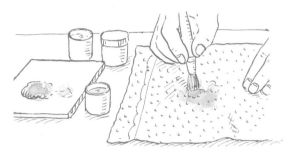

2. Dab the holes in the stencil, overlapping the edges. You need the lightest touch as pale flecks are enough.

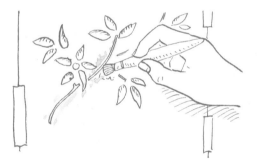

3. Colours can be blended on the stencil, or you can apply another layer of the same colour to get a darker shaded effect on one part of the stencil.

USING CRAYONS

Crayons are worked into a circle of colour on the tile or stencil and daubed with a brush as above. You can use the colour directly because it is not as thick as paint – there is no need to dab the brush on to kitchen paper.

USING SPRAY PAINT

1. Sprays take some practice and the stencil needs to be masked. Start the spray action to one side of the design, and work across in one direction so that the actual gap is filled during the middle of a paint spray. Otherwise use a card shield, spraying that rather than the stencil, so that it is the overflow of paint mist that floats on to the stencil. This will give a very subtle effect.

2. Colour is built up in layers of spray paint, as for liquid paints. By using the shield you can control the spray quite carefully and allow the different colours to overlap and merge for a three-dimensional effect.

Using Stencils as Borders and Papers

The more inspiration you seek for stencil designs and different ways of applying them, the more ideas and interpretations you will come across. Stencils can be used as wallpaper over an entire wall, as borders around the edge of it, as panels to break up a large area or as garlands to soften straight lines. The tricky part lies in choosing appropriately for the space you want to decorate. You might have to consider whether to put borders all around the doors and windows, above the skirting boards, chair rail or picture rail, or just around specific panelled areas to enhance pictures. Will you stencil in a recess, or only between the chair and picture rail, forming a deep frieze?

Stencilling on walls and ceilings can affect the perceived size or shape of the room, and as such can be used to advantage. For example, a very tall room with high ceilings will benefit from a border-style treatment at skirting board height and along the chair rail, bringing attention down the wall and so lowering the focus of the room. A border along the picture rail and chair rail will have a similar effect. High ceilings in halls and stairways also benefit from a low-level treatment, such as a border up the staircase wall at floor height. Conversely, a low ceiling is helped if it is painted the same colour as the walls and a stencilled border placed 10–15 cm (4–6 in) below ceiling height as a mock picture rail. The eye tends to imagine a standard-depth picture rail, so the illusion of a higher ceiling is created from the continuous border. On large blank expanses of wall, stencilled panels break up the area into smaller sections and provide a natural framework for pictures or lighting. In a smaller room, covering the whole area in a widely spaced stencil as a mock wallpaper with a light and soft colour combination can make the walls recede and lend the room a light, airy, spacious atmosphere.

Colours are important, not least because they can determine the mood of the room. Broken colour techniques used as a background work very well with stencilling: each motif ends up with a stippled, hand-finished look, so the background and foreground complement each other beautifully. Dark colour washes with a dense, opaque stencil in the same colour can look subtle and rich, as there is no clear contrast. The effect is a deepening of the regular stencilled design on a translucent random background. Stippling and soft ragging on also work well, and plain colour backgrounds can provide strong or subtle contrast depending on the colours you choose.

Roller stripes in contrast lines can be interrupted with stencils, either placed randomly or set along every other stripe to look like a wallpaper. Stripes in different shades of blue with gold or silver stars scattered over them, or pastel plaids sprinkled with shells and starfish, can transform a dull corner or recess.

For applying stencils as borders or wallpapers, the secret is to measure up the wall, using chalk and a plumbline, chalk string or a spirit level (see pp. 84–5). Start from the centre point and work outwards, so that you have an equal number of patterns on each side and any clever fitting is done at the corners. You can then complete the measuring up guides using a stencil template.

Roller stripes have been separated by equal-width spaces to enable a flower stencilled border to be used vertically.
The overall effect is that of hand-made wallpaper.

Stencilling is intended to have a hand-made quality, so there is no need to be too rigid in the layout. A certain freehand style is appealing and appropriate, especially on soft floral shapes or ribbon trails, although more geometric designs can be unpleasant to look at if they are not evenly spaced.

Nevertheless, there are a few guidelines which are worth following. Spend a little time measuring up the wall so that you do not have to think about where to place the stencil when you are working. If you are making a stencilled paper or border using lining paper, measure up the wall and cut out the lining paper first, so that you only stencil what you need. See Chapter 7 for working with papers and patterns, as the stencil designs on the lining paper might need to be treated as a regular pattern drop.

For large designs, those with many repetitions and extensive areas of stencilled motifs, consider using an aerosol, roller or decorating sponge. The aerosol will reveal the finest detail in the stencil whereas the sponge or roller might not. Use the latter for larger, less intricate designs where they have the added advantage of being faster and easier than a brush. However, if the brush finish created by fine stippling is the particular effect that you want to achieve, use a larger paintbrush such as a stippling brush rather than a small stencilling brush.

How to Mark Up a Stencilled Border

MATERIALS

- Spirit level, chalk string or plumbline
- Chalk or chinagraph pencil
- Step ladder
- Cleaning materials such as sugar soap
- Stencil
- Card
- Scissors, craft knife or hole punch
- Pencil

HINTS

Wipe off the stencil at regular intervals with an appropriate solvent to prevent the holes from clogging.

For best results, try out your ideas on lining paper first. Indeed, you can actually make your panels or borders on the lining paper if it proves easier than working up a ladder directly on to a wall. You simply add another stage to the process, as the finished result needs to be hung like wallpaper or a ready-made border (see Chapter 7).

PREPARATION

Make sure the surface is clean and dry – if you are using a special paint effect underneath, it must be dry or the stencil may damage the surface. If the wall is to be painted use emulsion or vinyl silk. Have as much access as possible to the entire area you are working on. Choose a relatively simple design that is a good size for a border, small enough to be repeated and not so small that it is lost or too fiddly to do. Decide where you are going to apply it and measure the design and check the spacing, marking out the guides with chalk.

TECHNIQUE

See Chapter 4 for details of how to apply different stencil paints and materials. These larger projects are easiest to do using an aerosol. When stencilling a border, try to avoid breaking the design off at the corner, and aim to make each corner the same.

1. Take the stencil and stick it temporarily to a piece of card. With a pencil draw around the whole stencil sheet, then draw a diagonal line through each corner, continuing on to the card. Draw a vertical and horizontal line intersecting at the centre. Cut out the stencil outline, putting a notch on each edge where the cross-lines intersect, and make a small hole at the centre point. This card is now your template.

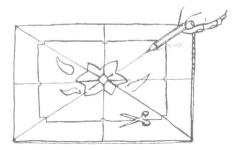

2. Find the centre of the wall or strip that you intend to border with stencils, and mark a point on that line to be the centre of the first motif. Lay the template on the wall so that the marks line up with the hole, and draw around the template.

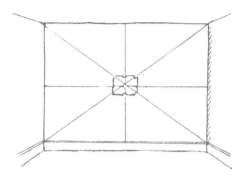

3. Using the spirit level from the middle of the central mark, draw a continuous line along the wall. This is your centre line guide. Take the template and use it to mark the centre point of the motifs around the wall, spacing them from the middle out.

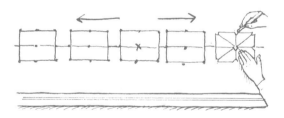

4. Use your eye to judge the right width between the stencils, and if possible set them to finish at or just before the corners. Otherwise use a small section of the stencil to fill in an unwanted gap at a corner.

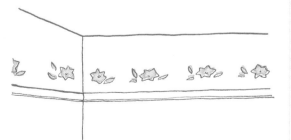

5. For a whole wall, use a plumbline to find the centre of the wall and work out from there. Some designs will need only a vertical guide. Do not worry if the motif is less than perfectly straight – the inaccuracy will add to the charm of the overall hand-done effect.

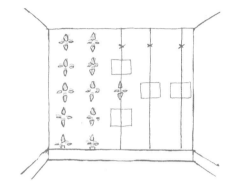

6. If you want to make a wallpaper effect the stencil needs to be quite accurately laid out. Spend some extra time marking up the wall, and use additional marker points in the stencil to line it up exactly with the template outline.

Stencils for Furniture and Fun

Stencilling need not be a serious process – the designs themselves and the places they are positioned can be light-hearted and humorous. Patterns and their positioning are a matter of shape and colour working together in harmony. However, recognisable objects such as animals and toys need to be considered slightly differently. They will work best wherever the real object would work. In other words a stencilled pot of flowers needs to 'stand' somewhere, and a stencilled hanging basket needs to 'hang'. A row of stencilled books or dolls works beautifully along the back edge of a shelf or table; fish, on the other hand, need to float free or crowd as they might do in shoals.

You have to consider each design individually on its own merits – and even some patterns work in only one way. A fleur-de-lys upside down will look as awkward as a hanging sunflower, whereas a blooming rose in isolation can be used almost as a pattern. These natural principles applied to walls or furniture will help make your stencils work visually.

Some stencils are made in more than one part and designed to be built up in sections of different colours, such as a trailing rose design, or growing fruits, where leaves and flowers and berries are stencilled separately. The easiest material for these is transparent acetate, so that each design can be seen through the next and lined up accordingly. Most stencil shops supply these with registration marks on the stencils. In any case, the individual leaves and flowers can be shaded just as they are in nature. Variegated leaves always have a lovely three-dimensional quality to them, whereas using one colour without variation in tone can sometimes look flat.

Take your time when planning smaller stencils. If they are to go on furniture it is worth using chalk or a chinagraph pencil to draw the stencil on the piece and see where the motif would look best. Centralise patterns on doors and chairs this way and stand back to judge whether it works or not.

There is no rule which says that any particular stencil must be accurately repeated in its entirety. Some can be used in different directions, reversed and turned to make them more versatile. They can be part of a freehand style – applied to the walls or woodwork with no guidelines at all, other than a feel for the sort of result you want. For example, if you had a stencil of three fish and some seaweed and shells you could repeat just the fish element over and over again. A single row of reeds and seashells appearing to grow up from the skirting board, the edge of a door or a window frame will appear to have shoals of fish swimming above them. Alternatively the fish could be used as an informal border, nosing their way up to the edge of the ceiling as if to the surface of a pool of water. In much the same way different flowers can be stencilled and grouped around a skirting board or chair rail as they might appear in a field or wood – naturally clumped in colours or types. Remember, stencils do not have to be used exactly as they are cut, or painted in a continuous line of repeated motifs.

If you are using stencils in this freehand way brushes are the easiest method of application as they give you greatest control over which area of the stencil to use. You can almost create *trompe-l'oeil* effects if the stencil is well drawn and carefully cut. Strictly speaking, *trompe-l'oeil* is a highly specialist effect where a 'trick of the eye' causes the viewer to wonder whether the image is real or not. Stencilling generally creates a soft, hand-made feel to the image which is delightful

Teddy bear and book stencils have been used in this child's room as a frieze which is almost a mural.
The colours are carefully mixed to give the bears and books a three-dimensional quality.

in its own right and does not pretend to be the real thing. However, some well-placed trails of ivy on the side or a garden shed, or a cat sitting on a windowsill, will make an attractive talking point without requiring the specialist skills of a professional *trompe-l'oeil* artist.

The actual stencil designs can be varied with shades of colour, which can be done just as effectively with an aerosol as with a brush. The key is to work in very fine layers. If you are using brushes, keep a separate brush for each colour and press it on to a tile or saucer and then on to kitchen paper first to make sure it is almost dry. You can then build up the colours and create tabby markings on the sitting cat, or tropical rainbow effects on the swimming fish.

How to Stencil Furniture

MATERIALS

- Stencils
- Chalks for trying out and placing the design
- Paper and masking tape to mask the furniture
- Paints
- Brushes if applicable, preferably one per colour
- Tile for liquid paint
- Kitchen paper

PREPARATION

Prepare your colours so that you can vary the tones of each design, shading the motifs or characters to give them a three-dimensional quality. If you are going to spray the stencil, make sure the furniture is well masked up.

TECHNIQUE

See the relevant previous project, depending on what type of paint you intend to use. Furniture with large flat areas, such as cupboards, can be sprayed. Small pieces are better controlled using a brush and liquid paints.

HINT
You can use a number of different stencils to build up a decoration based on an overall theme. For instance, a colourful circus scene could be created from individual stencils of clowns, performing animals, jugglers and flags.

1. Find the right position for your stencil by playing around with it and using chalk to 'sketch' the right place.

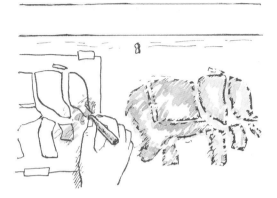

2. Imagine a light source to one side of the shape that gets gradually darker through the tones.

3. If it is a flat pattern, consider making the edges darker or lighter all around or to one side, as shown in the picture opposite.

4. Alternatively, the first colour can be applied more evenly all over the stencil.

5. Adding layers carefully to create darker parts, you will achieve a delightful three-dimensional quality.

6. For multi-part stencils you can work in the same way, building up sections of the design with layers of colour to form shading.

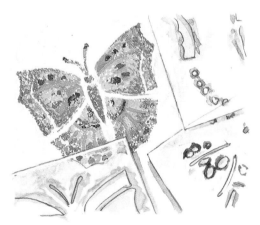

Alternative Ideas

STENCILLED GLASS

Stencils are usually quite colourful – however, they can look wonderful in metallic paints or plain white, especially on glass. It is possible to stencil glass quite densely and give it the appearance of having been frosted. This is an excellent way of creating a screen, or covering a window without shutting out the light directly. The stencilling itself can be done in much the same way as a coloured stencil, with the edges darker or lighter and the same three-dimensional effect of layering the tones. Glass fronted cupboards can be stencilled instead of having a fabric back, and even the edges of a mirror or corners of a window can be decorated simply in this way.

STENCILS AND TROMPE-L'OEIL

Stencils can be applied to so many surfaces and used in so many ways that even the garden can be decorated with them tastefully. A back wall stencilled with sunflowers or the side of a house covered in painted hanging baskets can be done with the same tongue-in-cheek humour as a trompe-l'oeil painting. In fact it works extremely well if you enhance existing flowers and plants by stencilling behind them. A window box of geraniums against a wall with more geraniums painted on to it, or terracotta pots overflowing with flowers – in both real and mural form – can work to stunning effect.

6
Murals

The word 'mural' comes from the French *mur* and broadly speaking it refers to a painting done directly on to a wall. There are many splendid examples of this highly acclaimed fine art form, such as Leonardo da Vinci's *The Last Supper*. Through the years, however, the mural has evolved to become a blanket term for any type of wall picture. Even graffiti can present a brilliant array of images and colours, and many cities boast some wonderful murals on the sides of buildings. They are usually bold and dramatic – in scale, if not in technical skill.

Painting figures and characters on walls goes back to primitive man, and simple yet stunning cave paintings such as the ones at Lascaux in France have survived for thousands of years. The walls of the ancient Egyptian pyramids reveal the rich history of earlier civilisations through beautiful drawings and hieroglyphics. Different techniques and cultural styles have evolved through time, although there is much to be said for the simple figurative style of the earliest artists and a great deal of inspiration can be found in books on ancient history and art.

Another type of mural that traditionally required an artist with consummate skills is *trompe-l'oeil*, which has already been mentioned in Chapter 5. Correctly done, a *trompe-l'oeil*

In this chapter:

- Short cuts to finer art
- Reproducing images
- Character mural
- Alternative ideas

painting will make you think you see something that is not there in reality. It may be a hat hanging on a wall, a view through a window or a door in a wall – when none of these really exist.

Trompe-l'oeil is interpreted a little more loosely today and overlaps mural painting and painted furniture. Success is found in the simplest ideas, designed as much to be humorous as artistically brilliant. Scaled down to fit the home, there is wide scope for different types of mural that are easy to do. For those who are not trained artists there are simple techniques for reproducing images and painting them in delightful ways.

Inspiration from books – from gardening books to nursery rhymes – provides an excellent source for a range of ideas, including the outlines you want to scale up. The key is to be able to reproduce your idea or original drawing to scale. Some of the ways of doing so are explained in this chapter.

Short Cuts to Finer Art

Murals and *trompe-l'oeil* give such wide scope to the imagination that it is difficult to keep all there is to say to a few short projects. Some people dismiss them as too difficult to consider, but such schemes can bring an element of fun to the decoration of a room, especially if it belongs to a child, and it is just that sense of humour that permits amateurs to have a go and enjoy themselves painting directly on to the walls.

The vast array of equipment and facilities available nowadays can make the possibilities seem overwhelming. The hardest part need not be the planning and painting but rather choosing what to do and how to carry it out. Even though it may take a professional artist to turn the stair wall into an authentic city skyline, it just takes patience to make a child's room exciting or add a touch of mural humour to a bathroom or staircase.

The main distinction between a mural and *trompe-l'oeil* is that the latter is always painted actual size and must be as real as possible so that the eye is literally tricked – however briefly – into thinking there really is a view beyond the window (or indeed a window at all). True *trompe-l'oeil* is very exacting and it takes an enormous amount of time and patience to paint objects and shadows in exact proportion, perspective and scale. However, a lot of artistic licence can be allowed in humorous murals that do not pretend to be real but nevertheless delight the eye.

Character murals are defined by an absence of background – the drawings or paintings are restricted to isolated images. A standard mural can be a picture that covers all or part of a wall and includes a background. It deserves a great deal of thought and preparation and is likely to take more time to complete than a character mural. However it need not be particularly difficult, and time spent preparing it and scaling it up will provide the best foundation for the finished painting.

Murals need not be sophisticated or true to life. A sea scene made up of sponged and stencilled fishes and potato-cut coral on a blue-green colour wash background can be as delightful as a bathroom transformed into an undersea world of exquisite dolphins and tropical fish. The latter may be hand-painted by an artist, but both decorative schemes work in the right place and the former may well bring the most joy if you and your children did it together.

Another way to treat a mural is as an ongoing project. A wall that is to be gradually transformed into a teddy bears' picnic, say, or a farmyard, can be slowly added to over time. Sponge-stamped leaves and flowers can be turned into trees to build up the background, while the animals can be painted and stippled or daubed with fluffy fabric to give them texture and shape. It can provide an endless source of fun with no need for sophisticated techniques or exacting drawing – even teddy bears or farm animals can come from stencils originally.

A background does not have to be traditional. A wall covered in brightly coloured balls as a background, with clowns spinning and tumbling all over it with no regard for 'normal' scale, can look great, as can a wall of clouds with aeroplanes, helicopters and hot air balloons painted over it. A mural can be very personal and entirely in your own style – usually the more confidence you have and the more pleasure you derive from creating it the better it looks!

This delightful mural has been built up with a host of nursery rhyme characters that look as if they are almost piled on top of each other. With an ambitious project like this, time and care go into the planning and patience into the painting.

How to Scale Up and Paint a Mural the Simple Way

MATERIALS

- Rough paper and tracing paper
- Coloured pens or pencils
- Scissors

} for trials and making original drawing

- HB pencil
- One or two fat black marker pens for outlines if required
- Plumbline and spirit level for scaling up
- Stencil (if that is your design source)
- Lining paper
- Acrylic paint in a range of colours
- Foil freezer trays or saucers for paint
- 1 cm (½ in) brushes for detail
- 2.5 cm (1 in) and 5 cm (2 in) household brushes
- Clean rags
- Clear polyurethane varnish if required

PREPARATION

Have a smooth emulsion surface to work on – vinyl silk is the favourite because it makes it easy to wipe clean and eliminate mistakes while the mural is wet. Do the full drawing, in colour, on rough paper as a colour guide. It may be helpful to photocopy it to a larger size to work from. Once the emulsion surface is dry you can make a background interesting by simply applying watered down emulsion (tinted, if you like, with acrylic colour) with a rag all over the wall.

TECHNIQUE

The technique you use will depend largely on the type of mural you decide to create and whether it is to be carefully and formally painted, or more light-hearted and created through a mixture of effects. Use water-based paints together on an emulsion background and experiment with different brush marks, rags and materials for the different effects you can achieve for backgrounds and foregrounds. Remember to keep the paler, bluer colours to the background, with low detail and stronger reds and yellows to the foreground where detail will not be lost. For example, a plain pale blue-green on a hill will work as a background to a strong, bright green foreground scattered with colourful flowers and textured to look like grass. This way colours that naturally come forward are balanced with those that naturally recede and you will achieve some depth in the picture.

Build up your picture with lots of individual animals or toys, cars or buildings placed together and linked into a scene with leafy trees or flowers – or coral, rocks and anemones if it is under water.

1. The traditional technique is to draw a rectangle to the same proportion as the wall and square it up on tracing paper that is laid over the drawing.

2. Mark up the wall using chalk and a spirit level, squaring it off the same as the drawing.

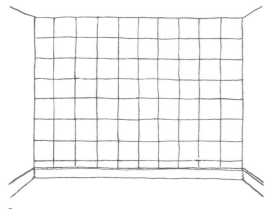

3. Copy each square from the drawing on to the wall until you have transferred the complete outline of your mural. Gradually add detail for different colours.

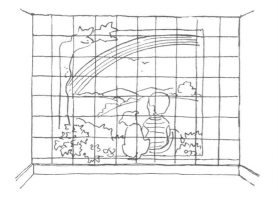

4. Depending on what you are doing, you can paint in pale patches of plain colour to denote different areas, such as blue for sky, green for grass and so on.

5. To this can be added various techniques – such as stamped or painted leaves, and stippled, sponged or stencilled flowers and foliage. Gradually build up your picture, filling in the different areas.

Reproducing Images

There are various practical ways to reproduce images for creating murals of any kind. An experienced artist might draw directly on to the wall – surprisingly enough, it can be easier to work on a large scale than bent over a piece of paper. However, a large expanse of wall can look very daunting, so you may prefer to take a piece of lining paper, flattened or pinned to a board.

Draw on the lining paper a rectangle in the same proportion as the wall. This way you have a mini-wall to work on and can spend time sketching or cutting out and sticking pictures together, until you have a basic design to work from. The paper provides freedom from worrying about making mistakes – if you decide you want to start again, it is easily discarded.

The traditional method of scaling up is to draw vertical and horizontal lines over your drawing, boxing it to match a similar framework drawn on to the wall, as shown on p. 99. But there are other methods available too: choose according to the type of mural you are setting out to do. The individual shapes of character murals (see p. 100) in particular can be transferred more simply.

One method is to draw the character in outline and enlarge it on a photocopier to the size you require. This may mean sticking more than one sheet together. Lay the drawing on to a medium-thick polystyrene (styrofoam) tile, and then use a knitting needle or skewer to push holes through the drawing at approximately 1 cm (½ in) intervals. Stick the drawing to the wall with masking tape and mark the holes with a pencil. You can then remove the drawing and join up the dots. This method works best for smaller individual images.

Depending on the size of the image, you can draw or photocopy it and trace it on to the wall by rubbing the back with a soft pencil or stick of charcoal and then drawing over the lines and pressing through the paper to make a replica drawing on the wall. Again, this method is best restricted to smaller images as it can leave lots of unwanted marks on the wall and can therefore be unmanageable on a large scale.

There is another method of accurate reproduction that involves some technical equipment. However, it works very well for large pictures and takes a lot of the difficulties out of scaling up and reproducing the picture in the traditional way. First, you need a photograph of your chosen image in transparency form. Then use a slide projector to project the image on to the wall, moving it back until it fills the space. If there is not enough room to go back far enough, project the image on to a large sheet of paper and scale up from there. You will need to balance the light in the room; it should be low enough to project the image reasonably clearly, and high enough for you to see where you are drawing. You simply take a pencil and draw around the shapes projected on to the wall.

Sometimes a transparency can provide a lovely background for you to cover with individual character murals afterwards. It may be possible to use the transparency as a colour guide as well – however, you may need to set up extra spot lighting to show your paint mixtures and obtain true colours.

Be careful not to let the image get too formal and literal. There is something very attractive about spontaneous paint marks and, while it helps to have a reliable base drawing, it can sometimes detract from the finished work if everything is too perfectly placed.

*Here a mural forms the background to some favourite toys and the room is like a stage set, with painted
trees standing proud of the wall and with real teddies hanging in them.*

How to Reproduce an Image

MATERIALS

Depending on the method you intend to use, the options are as follows:

- Lining paper
- Coloured pens
- Coloured pencils
- Scissors and glue
- Masking tape and a board

} for preparing your picture

- Photocopier
- Sticky tape if pages need sticking together
- Knitting needle or skewer
- Polystyrene (styrofoam) tiles
- HB pencil

- Chalk
- Plumbline
- Spirit level
- T-square

} for transferring the scale grid to the wall

- Slide projector
- Transparency of your chosen design
- Small table lamp if required
- Clean damp rag to wipe off pencil drawing mistakes

PREPARATION

Prepare the wall by having a clean emulsion surface in the base colour. Use vinyl silk, from which mistakes can be easily washed off while the mural paint is wet. Prepare your drawing by sticking lining paper flat to a board and drawing the outline of the wall in proportion, so that your finished design is made to the same scale.

TECHNIQUE

A mural is usually drawn with a pencil, which can be readily wiped off a vinyl silk surface with a damp cloth as long as it is done fairly soon. It is also pale enough to be hidden by the paint. Do not make the marks too heavy if you are using light-coloured paint, or the graphite will discolour it slightly. If it helps – and suits the type of mural you are doing – you can go over the outline with a thick permanent marker pen. (Do not use a water-based one, which will leak into the paint and discolour it.) Make sure it is dry before you start applying any paint on top. You may need to go over it again, at the end, where paint has overlapped the edges.

1. Create your image on the board, working to the same proportions as the wall. Ensure that all the colours and outlines are in place.

2. Scale the picture by drawing a grid over it, or on tracing paper laid over the top. It can then be transferred to a chalk grid (see p. 95).

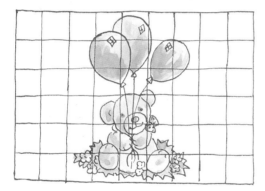

3. For a character mural photocopy the outline, enlarging it to the size you want (see p. 96).

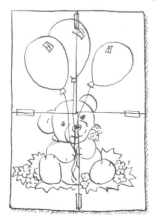

4. Lay the paper on to a polystyrene tile and punch holes with the knitting needle or skewer at regular intervals. Hang the picture on the wall and draw lightly through the holes, leaving marks on the wall to give the outline shape.

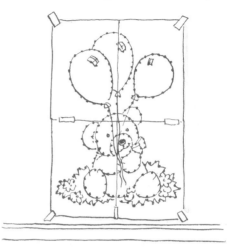

5. Join the dots to make a full outline. This method can be combined with others so that the characters have a background, which can be produced from plain paint and a rag or bright squares or circles, or by the more elaborate method using a projector which is described on p. 96.

Character Mural

Character murals, which have been alluded to in the previous two projects, are great fun. The first thing to do is decide where they are to go and how much space the characters are to take up. The difference between these and a more elaborate picture that takes up a whole wall is that no background of any kind is required. You can place all sorts of characters quite haphazardly over the walls without bothering too much about composition.

For the characters themselves there is an almost endless source of ideas for children's rooms in books and cartoon stories: Rupert Bear, Mickey Mouse and Peter Rabbit are just three of the more obvious ones. Cartoon books and magazines can also provide excellent drawings to work from in the scaling up process, and their simple outlines are relatively easy to reproduce.

Although character murals have no background they work best if they interact with other elements in the room. For example, a favourite animal from a children's story might be painted to look as if it is sitting on the end of your child's bed, or a string of balloons might float up from the corner of a cot. Birds or butterflies work best if they are positioned high on a wall, or as if settled on a window or picture frame. Clowns will walk or tumble to optimum effect if they have an edge to work on – peering around the side of a doorway, with only half the figure drawn, as if looking round it, or else dancing across the top of a radiator. Groups of animals and living images, like boats, cars and planes, need a 'working surround'. In other words, something that climbs will work best painted with something to climb on – a colourful snake, for instance, needs to be wrapped around a corner or sliding along a shelf or hanging down from the top of a cupboard.

Stencils are one of the simplest ways to create a character mural. They can be used 'straight' or to provide guidelines for a more detailed picture with added touches of your own. You can use the scaling up method to make a favourite design bigger if required. Do not work too small or with too much detail at first. Simple images will help you build up confidence and provide the impetus to experiment with painting techniques and gradually to get more ambitious.

Other images can be used and reproduced in various ways, as in the previous project. The key, particularly if you are scaling up accurately, is to do the preparation work thoroughly.

Find a finished picture to work from, or plan your design on paper. Bear in mind that detail is easily lost from a distance and few walls are viewed from closer than 1m (3 ft). You can use this to your advantage: the effect of roundness, for instance, is readily created with a few brush strokes. Most images will stand a three-dimensional touch. Bows and ribbons, flowers and balloons more interesting if built up with extra colours – there are tips for doing this in the project on p. 102.

The easiest materials to work with for this type of painting are acrylic paint on an emulsion background. They are both water-based and quite forgiving in terms of correction and cleaning up spills. An artist's supply shop will have a wide range of colours ready mixed in bottles. You will need two or three 1 cm (½ in) brushes for small-scale work and a range of small household brushes for the larger areas – whatever you are most comfortable with. There is an element of trial and error about mural painting – and some pleasant surprises too, when something works well in a way you might

This simple character mural moves into the humorous realm of trompe-l'oeil as it has been carefully painted life-size.
Add your own cheeky blue-tit.

not have expected. Keep standing back from your work as you paint, because the effect on a wall can be very different from a small image on paper – the scale alone creates impact.

Be careful not to work too small – tiny ribbons and bows in pale colours high up on a wall will be lost, but a huge butterfly splashed with primary colours will work much better. Work to actual size on lining paper first if it helps you, sticking your draft ideas on to the wall in order to position them well. It is

extremely helpful to do a rough colour version of your picture, so that you can use it as a guide and almost 'colour by numbers' on to the wall.

Where paint colours are concerned, have at least the primaries and white so that you can mix secondary colours. Once you get into the swing of it, two shades (one dark and one light) of each colour will provide you with all the scope you need for colour variation. Disposable foil freezer trays are excellent for holding paint and mixing colours.

How to Do a Character Mural

MATERIALS

- Rough paper and tracing paper
- Coloured pens or pencils
- Scissors

} for trials and making your original drawing

- HB pencil
- One or two fat black marker pens for outlines if required
- Plumbline and straight edge for scaling up
- Stencil (if that is your design source)
- Lining paper
- Acrylic paint in a range of colours
- Foil freezer trays or saucers for paint
- 1 cm (½ in) brushes for detail
- 2.5 cm (1 in) and 5 cm (2 in) household brushes
- Clean rags
- Clear polyurethane varnish if required

PREPARATION

Have a smooth emulsion surface to work on, preferably vinyl silk as it is easy to wipe clean and eliminate mistakes while the mural is wet. Do the full drawing, in colour, on rough paper as a colour guide. Reproduce the outlines of your drawing on the wall in pencil, either by scaling it up, tracing it on to the wall or drawing around a shape or stencil (see the instructions on scaling up a picture on pp. 94–5).

TECHNIQUE

The painting technique is simple in that you can paint haphazardly in different directions for one effect, or carefully in one direction for another. Choose one and stick to it, working with quite thick paint. This will give easy coverage, whereas diluted paint would drip and run. It will also produce strong opaque colours.

You can add some roundness with dark and light shades of your colours. Add some white to your colour for the mid-tone, use it neat for a darker shade, and add some colour to pure white for the palest tone. Imagine a single light source, so that darker shades will be on one side and lighter ones on the other. Textures, pattern and fur can be added by using a tiny amount of paint on a very dry brush to obtain a soft, fluffy finish, feathering off at the edges. Experiment with rags, cloths and paper to get different patterns too. Finally, the mural can be varnished for protection.

HINT
When mixing colours to obtain darker and lighter shades, make up small amounts and only add a little at a time to change the base colour gradually.

---

1. Having transferred your drawing to the wall in pencil, clean off any unwanted pencil marks and refer to your finished picture colour guide. Softly mark out colours on the wall if it helps.

2. Apply the basic colours to the wall, keeping the outlines as neat as possible by painting them with the side of the brush. But do not worry about this too much because brush marks tend not to show at a distance.

3. Balloons and other round shapes can be given a three-dimensional quality by the simple addition of a white highlight. This can be a neat cartoon-style shape, or a soft brush stroke, depending on what you are painting.

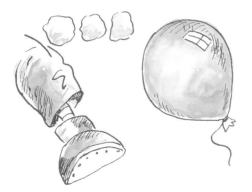

4. If it is in keeping with the style of your picture, you can draw on the outline and other features with a fat marker pen after the paint is dry. Alternatively these can be painted in black paint using a narrow brush, but it is much trickier to get an even outline.

Alternative Ideas

MURAL VIGNETTES

*Instead of painting whole walls and instead of using
known characters for character murals, you can
work with simple scenes or vignettes by adding only
a little background to the immediate surround. Make
the drawing a size that suits you to work with
comfortably – about 30–60 cm (1–2 ft) high. It is
worth taking the time to draw or trace the figures
carefully and select a simple line that will indicate
background. Here a small leafy branch is used for
an owl, bamboo for a panda and so on. A hot air
balloon might be finished with a few clouds or a boat
with some waves. Little scenes such as these work
well on small areas of walls, or panels, and – as
they are manageable – can be a good way to
experiment with colour before taking on larger
projects. They can be used in quite amusing ways
too. It is easy to reverse the image at the tracing
stage so that a pair of tigers can be painted sitting at
either end of a shelf. If you are feeling ambitious,
and it suits the room, they can be painted larger on
either side of a doorway.*

7
Working with Paper

Papering can appear a daunting prospect. It need not be. It requires some patience and time, but if you follow the procedures step-by-step it is relatively straightforward. By giving the required attention to the appropriate stages you can cut out many of the pitfalls.

Preparation of the foundation upon which you are going to paper is the crucial element. Otherwise problems may arise weeks after the job is completed – when the paper begins to peel off the wall. Time spent preparing the surfaces and the paper is as important as matching patterns and hanging the paper straight. This chapter gives the right professional instructions for all the different techniques involved. However, it is essential to follow the preparation and pasting instructions given in Chapter 2 (see pp. 21–4). Whether you are lining walls for papering or for painting, or papering directly on to the wall surface, the quality of the result will depend largely on the foundation. Some papers and most paint effects highlight any surface blemishes and discrepancies,

so the preparatory work is all-important.

This chapter provides straightforward instructions that aim to prevent these difficulties. The projects include basic papering as well as separate step-by-step instructions for papering around doors, windows and other obstructions. These methods are simple and reliable and include lots of the secrets used in the trade to get really professional-looking results.

In this chapter:

- Just borders
- Straight and simple panelling
- Hanging straight drops
- Papering around corners
- Papering around a doorway
- Papering around a light switch
- Papering around a radiator
- Papering around a window
- Hanging lining paper

Just Borders

Borders come in a variety of patterns and widths. They usually accompany a toning wallpaper design, but there is no reason why they cannot be used alone, with either a special paint effect or a plain paint colour. They can be used on a textured surface much as a stencilled border might, or simply used to surround or frame windows, doorways and wall edges. There is nothing to say that borders must be restricted to forming neat horizontal strips around the room. Sloping ceilings can be emphasised by narrow borders taken around all the corners, while stair walls can be transformed with an elegant border all the way up the skirting board, following the line of the stairs.

Borders also provide the perfect break between paint and wallpaper, or between two different paper patterns. Modern textiles and furnishings love mixing plaids and flowers or elaborate patterns with simple bold stripes in clever colour combinations. Borders can be used to marry the different shapes and bring the decor together – linking successfully with matching soft furnishings.

Children's rooms can be decorated simply but effectively by painting the walls in bright strong colours and adding a band of border paper all the way around. Some borders have self-adhesive backing, and colourful trails of animals, toys, cars and boats are readily available.

Another way of creating a border, particularly for a room with a high ceiling, is to cut out a patterned wallpaper in a repeating shape and hang it down from the picture rail or ceiling. If the same paper is used between the skirting board and chair rail, a delightful effect is created. It is also a clever way to use up all the off-cuts from the paper.

Consider the width and pattern of borders as well as their colouring when you are choosing them, and whether you want to make more of a feature or less. Used as panels, borders can replace beading and become frames for pictures or sections of wallpaper. Wide borders can be hung around the top and sides of a window instead of a pelmet or valance and prevent a roller or roman blind from looking too plain. Borders can be used for understatement or emphasis, and are a wonderfully versatile option to finish off all kinds of decorative paint and papering techniques.

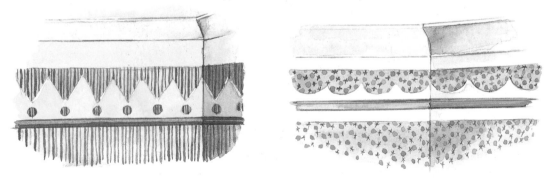

Creating a border from off-cuts of patterned wallpaper.

This bathroom has been decorated in plain paint, with a border used just to frame the window and link in with the blind and screen fabric.

How to Paste and Mitre a Border

MATERIALS

- Border paper
- Tacks, small hammer and string
- Spirit level
- HB pencil
- Metal ruler
- Appropriate glue or paste
- Craft knife with disposable blades
- Plastic spatula or soft cloth
- Damp sponge

PREPARATION

Decide where you are going to position the border. If there is no edge such as a door frame or picture rail to place it against, mark up guides before you start. For verticals use a plumbline and mark the wall with an HB pencil. For horizontals use two small tacks and a piece of string. Only place the tacks where the border will hide the holes. Put in the first tack and adjust the position of the second one with a spirit level. Draw a light pencil line as a guide.

HINT
Borders that are not self-adhesive can be stuck with standard wallpaper paste unless they are to be stuck on to vinyl wall coverings. In this case you must use commercial border adhesive or vinyl overlap adhesive.

1. Cut the border to the lengths you require, plus 5 cm (2 in) beyond the maximum possible length.

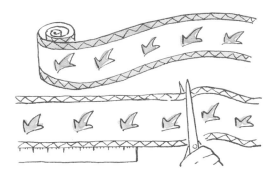

2. Paste and pleat each length for easy handling – concertina the piece back and forth with a soft fold. If it is self-adhesive, roll it the wrong way to get it flatter and work gradually, peeling the back off as you go. Do not remove it all at once.

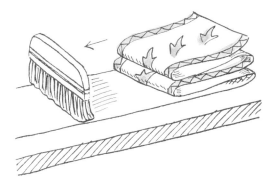

3. Use a plastic spatula or soft cloth to smooth the border into place, leaving the ends to overhang so that the next angle crosses over.

4. To mitre the corners, take a metal ruler and hold it at 45 degrees out from the corner. Take a sharp new blade and cut with gentle, repeated pressure until the blade cuts through both layers.

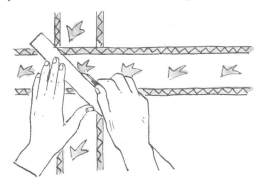

5. When the knife has cut through the two overlapping pieces, lift up and remove the cut pieces. Firmly stroke the mitred border into place, using a damp sponge to remove any surplus paste.

6. On long walls you may have to join lengths of border together. Cut the ends squarely and butt them up to each other, making sure the pattern matches.

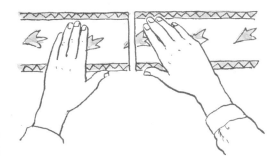

Straight and Simple Panelling

Paper hanging is something of a skill, and covering a whole room on your first attempt is quite ambitious. Handling a pattern drop and hanging the paper straight can become more complex as you cut in around doorways and windows and other obstacles such as radiators and light fittings. You must also know where to start to avoid patterns mismatching at a focal point in the room.

An easier option to begin with – and a beautiful decorative effect in its own right – is to mix paint and paper and create panels around the room. Another way is to paper only one section of the wall, such as the space between the skirting board and the chair rail. The reason for doing this is not necessarily to make the papering easier, although that is an advantage. It provides a number of successful decorative options that can affect the proportions of the room.

Dividing up walls needs to be done carefully, taking into account the amount and type of furniture and the shape of the room. It can look very busy if too much is added – although, by contrast, panelling can create space if it is thoughtfully placed. Panelling is a way to deal with both plain rectangular room shapes and awkward-angled rooms. Small sections of wall can have a narrow panel, if the paper design is suitable. Large wall spaces can be divided into more than one panel. By painting the surrounding wall and ceiling in the same colour, interest is focused on the panel. With the right use of colour, the sense of space can be manipulated.

To help create a feeling of spaciousness, choose a paper with a pale background and use a similar colour to paint the wall surrounding the panel. For a stronger effect, use darker or brighter colours selected from those in the paper design. Bear in mind that a stark contrast between the overall effect of the paper and the finished colour on the surrounding wall will create an illusion of the panel 'jumping out' at you, which can make the room appear smaller. On the other hand a white wall, with papered panels that have a white background, will reflect light and look bigger. Ivories and pastels have a similar effect and this treatment works very well in halls and stairways because of the light, airy feel it can create. A dramatic effect can be had from doing the same with dark colours. A rich blue and green tartan paper, hung in panels with walls painted in the blue and all the paintwork in green to match the beading of the panel, will look dark, strong and sophisticated in the right room. The panels can then be made into more of a feature, with pictures and picture lights hung in them. Treat the room as a whole rather than choosing the paper for the panels in isolation, so that you blend the colours and paper designs together to achieve an overall effect.

Chair rails and picture rails are another way of dividing walls effectively, and can be created with borders as well as the more traditional beading. You can use a wide border at chair rail height with a large patterned paper below and a narrow border at the picture rail, over a much smaller and more subtle pattern. There are unlimited possibilities, and each one works if the paper is hung well and simply merges into a background that is easy on the eye.

A popular treatment for the section between the chair rail and the skirting board is to hang an embossed paper, mimicking the style of the traditional Victorian Lincrusta. This can be painted to match or contrast with the surrounding woodwork. It can also look

Panels and borders have been used together here in an unusual treatment which makes them look like pictures. The principle is identical for a painted wall, where the panel only is papered.

stunning if it is treated with a special paint effect by distressing the embossed design once it has been painted. In this case the paper is painted with eggshell paint as described in Chapter 3 (see p. 52).

You can also hang embossed papers in panels and distress them, letting colour and texture form the basis of the decoration. These can work particularly well with soft furnishings in damasks that have the same textural quality and subtle patterning. If the same muted colour is used throughout the room, such panels can help give a sense of space but without letting the decoration become monotonous. Again, these panels provide the perfect backdrop for pictures and can be very successful even when made quite small, just to surround paintings well placed around the room.

How to Make a Panel

MATERIALS

- Beading
- Strong wood glue
- Mitre saw
- Primer
- Paint for woodwork
- 1 cm (½ in) paintbrush

PREPARATION

Measure up the walls so that the panels will all be the same height. Mark the panels out. The width can vary according to the shape of the room, but they should all have the same top and bottom level. If you can, make the width of the panels equal to a number of widths of wallpaper to reduce the amount of trimming you will have to do.

TECHNIQUE

To make panels or rails successfully you must plan the layout carefully and draw up the wall or walls accurately, numbering each side as you go. This gives you a good guide to work from, so that once the plan is completed you are free to concentrate on each panel.

The second essential is to get good-quality beading and mitre the corners as neatly as possible. Number each length according to your plan and check that adjacent pieces fit together well at the corners before you fix them. Buy beading that is flat and as far as possible knot-free. If you are using a lot of beading and some knots are unavoidable, they must first be treated with knotting solution. If you fail to do so, after the panel is fixed and painted sap may leak from it and spoil your work.

HINTS
You can trim the side and front edges of shelving with beading to match the style of panels or chair and picture rails.

If you decide to put a special paint effect inside a panel, which is to overlap on to the beading itself – or if you wish to distress the beading (see p. 53) – it is a good idea to varnish it. Use a clear gloss or mid-sheen varnish once everything is dry and before you have removed any masking from outside the panel. This will help to protect it.

1. Measure the panel on the wall and draw it with a metal ruler, using a spirit level for the horizontal and vertical lines. Mark exactly where the outside edge has to go.

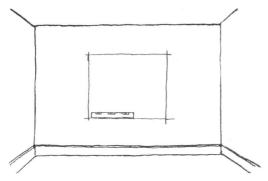

2. Cut the four pieces of beading to size, making each end cut at 45 degrees so that the corners are perfectly mitred. Using a good mitre saw will avoid the need for filling the corners.

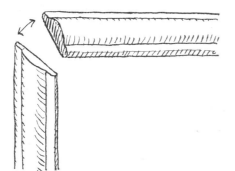

3. Place a generous amount of wood glue along the length of the top piece of beading. While the glue is wet, press the beading gently to the wall where it will be attached and then remove it, leaving a line of glue correctly placed on the wall.

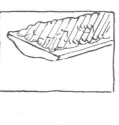

4. Wait for the glue to go tacky on both the wall and the beading (usually five minutes – see the instructions on the glue). Then attach the beading to the wall. This simple method avoids mess as glue is only applied where it is needed.

5. Mask all around the outside edge of the beading, if it is to be painted a different colour from the surrounding wall. In any case, prime the beading with primer, then apply one coat of eggshell paint. (If there are any knots in the beading they must be treated first with knotting solution.) Paint a top coat on to the beading. Let this dry completely before papering inside the panel. If you intend to use a paint effect, such as distressing, inside the panel, then you can give the beading the same treatment.

Professional Papering Techniques

Papering need not be as difficult as it seems, if time and care are taken to prepare the surfaces and to measure up the spacing (see pp. 21–4 and 32–3). You will find that by preparing paper in batches you develop a rhythm of working. Obstacles such as light switches, radiators, door and window frames are often daunting prospects. However, taken one step at a time, and following the straightforward professional guidelines given in this chapter, they can be successfully papered without hassle. To start with, choose smaller patterns or plainer papers as they are easier to work with. Large patterns tend to be less forgiving because mistakes and mismatches are usually more obvious.

One of the questions to be considered is whether or not to line a wall with plain lining paper. Lining a wall serves more than one purpose: it both conceals surface blemishes and acts as an excellent base on which to paste papers or paint special effects. If you intend to hang wallpaper on top, walls can be lined horizontally. However, If you plan to do paint effects the walls are better lined vertically (as you would normally hang wallpaper) before being painted with the base colour.

Lining papers are available in various weights which are selected by professional decorators for a number of different reasons. However for most purposes, and particularly for special paint effects, all you need is one layer of heavy-duty lining paper, gauge 1200.

For lining a wall before carrying out a special paint effect, treat the lining paper exactly as if it was wallpaper and turn to p.116 for details. The pasting and hanging techniques are the same, although the cutting is easier because no pattern matching is involved.

Horizontal hanging for a wall that is to be papered afterwards should not be confused with what is known as cross lining. Strictly speaking, cross lining is so called because two layers of light- to medium-gauge lining paper are hung – the first vertically and the second horizontally – before the wallpaper is put up vertically. It is rarely an advantage to cross line a wall for anything but the most specialised wall coverings.

Details of how to hang lining paper horizontally are given on p. 126. Whichever way you are hanging it, the secret of the success is to hang the paper within approximately ½ cm (¼ in) of the edges of the wall, skirting, coving or other boundary. You subsequently take the wallpaper itself over the lining paper, right to the edges. This means that the wallpaper is attached directly to the wall at this point and the vulnerable edges are sealed. Even if the edge of the lining paper starts to lift off, if this method has been used it should not take the wallpaper with it. Also, if the edge of the wallpaper lifts, it can easily be repaired.

HINT
When patching wallpaper, gently tear it rather than cutting with a knife or scissors. Tearing creates a softer edge which will join invisibly.

A simple colour scheme ensures that the mixture of paint, paper, borders and fabrics works beautifully together in this child's room

Simple Hanging of Straight Drops

MATERIALS

- Pasted wallpaper
- Wallpaper brush
- Plastic spatula
- Damp sponge
- Apron with pockets
- Metal scraper
- Sharp craft knife with snap-off blades
- Metal ruler
- Step ladder

PREPARATION

This method is used where there are no obstructions, and it is the basic technique that applies to all papering. See Chapter 2 for details of preparing to paper and pasting up.

Having chosen the wall to start on, paste up the paper required for that wall. The first piece should have soaked sufficiently by the time you have completed the pasting (check this with the manufacturer's advice on the paper you have purchased).

TECHNIQUE

Remember to work as cleanly as possible when hanging wallpaper. Reverse roll it to help alleviate the problem of curling. Cover the pasting table with lining paper and keep the paper slightly overhanging when pasting. This will prevent the paste going on to the table and marking the surface of the paper (see p. 34). Wear an apron with pockets so that you can keep your spatula, brush and craft knife with you all the time. Besides a damp sponge for leaking seams, it is also very useful to have one or two damp cloths to hand for wiping sticky fingers as you work.

HINT

If you are putting up washable vinyl paper in a room with a damp atmosphere like a bathroom or kitchen use a fungicidal paste to prevent mould growing beneath it.

1. From the instructions on pp. 32–6 you will have marked up the wall and pasted the paper, ready to hang, in numbered sequence. Carry the first pasted roll carefully up the ladder.

2. Unroll the paper and peel one end apart, sticking it in place so that there is a 5 cm (2 in) overlap at the top. Ensure it runs down your plumbline.

3. Taking the plastic spatula, smooth the paper gently and firmly away from you as if with brush strokes. The spatula will even the distribution of paste and smooth the edges at the same time without the need for a seam roller. Repeat for the lower half of the wall with the remaining paper.

4. If the paper is embossed, use the wallpaper brush to brush it gently into place without crushing the embossing. If there are bubbles, peel back the paper and brush back into the fold until it is flat. (If you are producing a lot of bubbles the paper has not soaked enough.)

5. Press the scraper into the crease at the top and bottom, scoring along the edge line of the fold. Holding the metal ruler firmly against the edge, cut through the paper with the craft knife (using a sharp new blade) for a clean straight line.

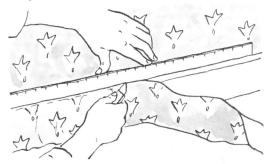

6. Repeat the process with the second piece, butting it up to the first piece and lining up the pattern if there is one. While the paste is wet, the paper will slide into place. Wipe leaking seams with the damp sponge.

How to Paper Around Corners

MATERIALS

- Pasted wallpaper
- Wallpaper brush
- Plastic spatula
- Damp sponge
- Apron with pockets
- Metal scraper
- Sharp craft knife with snap-off blades
- Metal ruler
- Step ladder

PREPARATION

Plan your room so that there is an overlap on both internal and external corners.

INTERNAL CORNER

1. Butt the paper up to the piece next to it and leave it to overlap the corner. Brush this firmly with the wallpaper brush or plastic spatula.

2. Peel the paper back and cut with the scissors so that you have a 6 mm (¼ in) overlap on to the next wall. To prevent puckering you can snip this on an internal corner, especially if the wall is uneven.

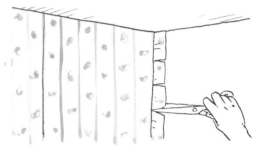

3. Plumb a line on the next wall so that the piece will overlap the first wall by 6 mm (¼ in), and hide the snipped piece underneath.

4. Brush firmly with the wallpaper brush or plastic spatula. Trim off excess into corner and continue on to the second wall.

EXTERNAL CORNER

1. Avoid having an edge down the corner, as it will be very vulnerable to becoming unstuck. Plan to take the paper around the corner with an overlap of at least 5 cm (2 in). Butt the next piece up to it.

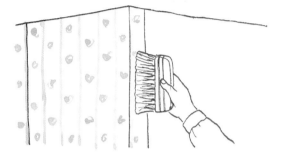

2. Alternatively you can overlap the next piece, leaving a 5 cm (2 in) overlap at the corner – but don't forget to plumb on the new wall. Fold and tear the second piece down its length to overlap the first piece. This gives a feathered edge and no hard line showing.

HINT
Using a decorating apron with a large front pocket enables you to keep essential tools such as wallpaper brush, spatula, craft knife and cloths with you all the time.

How to Paper Around a Doorway

1. A typical doorway can have one width of paper above it. During your planning stage aim for this to be in the middle above the door if possible.

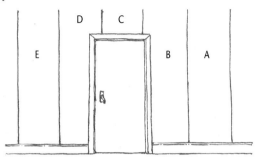

2. Hang piece B, butting it up to piece A top to bottom. Let the left edge which meets the door flap over it.

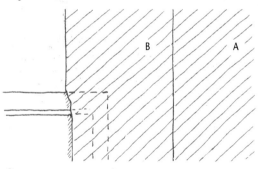

3. Using your plastic spatula, flatten the paper right up to the side of the door frame and make a crease. When you can feel the top of the door frame, make a diagonal snip with the scissors. Carefully tear the last 6 mm (¼ in) to the corner.

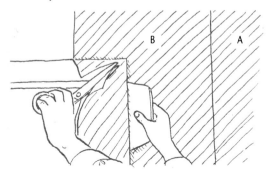

4. Crease into the top and side of the door frame and score with the metal scraper. Holding the metal ruler into the edges, cut with the craft knife to make a neat edge.

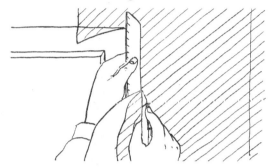

5. If the paper snags during cutting, replace the knife blade. Then gently press the paper back in place with your finger. Cut again against the metal ruler in the opposite direction.

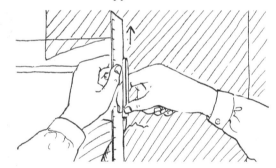

6. The reason for tearing the last 6 mm (¼ in) to the corner is that a snip will create a sharp line, but a small tear will mend invisibly.

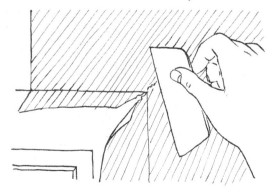

By planning the papering carefully it can be done seamlessly around doorways and other obstructions.
Papers without distinct pattern drops, such as these which are designed to look like paint effects, are the easiest.

How to Paper Around a Light Switch

PREPARATION

Turn off the electricity or isolate the power to the light switch. Then unscrew the panel enough to create a 1 cm (½ in) gap behind it.

1. Paper the wall from the top down as normal, going over the light switch but without sticking the paper down below the switch plate.

2. Feel for the light switch in the middle and pinch the glued paper as near to the centre of the switch as possible. Snip to create a space in which to insert the lower edge of the scissors.

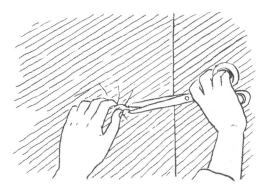

3. Using the scissors, make small cuts from the centre to near the corners of the light switch. Smooth the paper on the wall either side of the switch to ensure you have the paper in position.

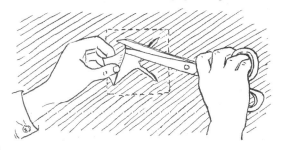

4. To ensure that the paper is lying flat around the switch, tear the last part at the corners. A snip always shows, but a small tear can be invisibly mended.

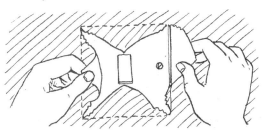

5. Trim off anything more than 1 cm (½ in) of paper that can be tucked behind the light switch.

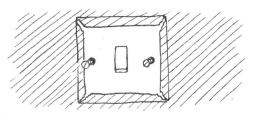

6. Use the spatula to tuck the allowance behind the switch plate. When the paper is flat screw the plate back into place, but not too tightly.

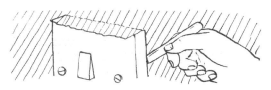

How to Paper Around a Radiator

MATERIALS

- As for simple hanging of straight drops (p. 116)
- Roller extension to get behind the radiator

PREPARATION

Turn off the radiator, even if it is winter. The heat will dry out the paper much too quickly and prevent it from sticking to the wall.

1. Assess carefully what can and cannot be seen behind a radiator. Typically you will want to paper 15–20 cm (6–8 in) in from all edges.

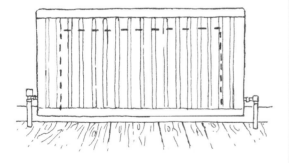

2. Line up the paper, while it is still folded together, over any brackets behind the radiator.

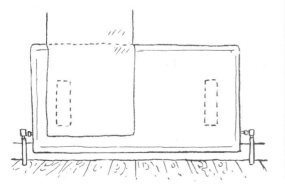

3. Unroll it as necessary in front of the radiator and cut a slit up from the bottom to go over the bracket, with two diagonals at the top.

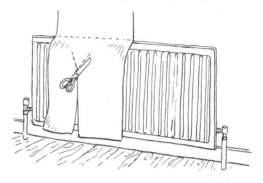

4. Using the roller, roll the paper in place down behind the radiator.

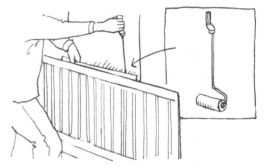

5. If the area under the radiator can be seen, cut and paste a full drop and cut off the bottom strip, placing it first. Then continue as step 4. As a general rule, ease paper behind a radiator where you can see plus 5 cm (2 in).

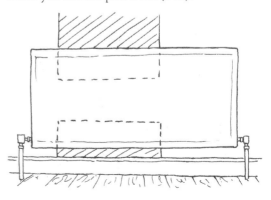

How to Paper Around a Window

MATERIALS

- Pasted wallpaper
- Wallpaper brush
- Plastic spatula
- Damp sponge
- Apron with pockets
- Metal scraper
- Sharp craft knife with snap-off blades
- Metal ruler
- Step ladder

1. In the planning stages, make sure you measure up so that there is a width of paper cut to cover the window reveal by the depth of the reveal plus 5 cm (2 in).

2. Cut a line 6 mm (¼ in) above the soffit down into the corner at 45 degrees. Leave the top piece in place as a guide. Cut the bottom piece in line with the window board.

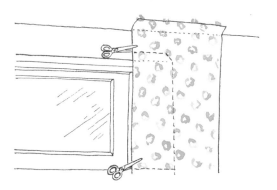

3. Fit to the reveal and trim, leaving the surplus 6 mm (¼ in) on the soffit. Do not cut away the shaded area yet. Although it will eventually become scrap it will first provide you with a guide for the next piece.

4. Take up the second piece of paper that will cover the soffit. Using the edge of the previous piece as a guide, hang this piece and fit and trim it to the soffit.

5. Cut away the scrap piece (shaded area), leaving 5 cm (2 in) waste. This will be cut away, but first the next piece will overlap it.

6. Cut a third piece of paper to the same size drop as the second piece, to cover the width of the shaded area plus 5 cm (2 in) allowance. Stick this piece butted up to the third piece (step 4) with patterns matching. Trim into the corner of the soffit and reveal and inside the window edge. It will overlap the scrap of the first piece.

7. With a metal ruler and a sharp knife, cut though both layers of paper from ceiling to soffit corner, in line with the reveal.

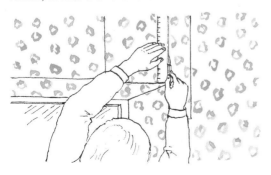

8. Peel back and remove the surplus paper from underneath the new piece and over the first piece, sponging off any excess paste. Repeat the other way around for the next corner.

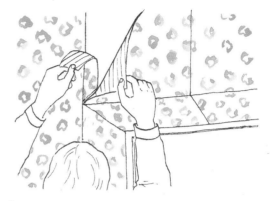

9. If you are using a heavily patterned paper, cut the excess to include a pattern and cut around the pattern to disguise even the usual seams. Bear in mind that window seams are sometimes hidden by curtains.

How to Hang Lining Paper

If you intend to paper over the lining paper, hang it within 6 mm (¼ in) of the edges and corners of walls, skirtings etc. Then take the wallpaper right to the edges (see p.114).

1. Plan the wall, using a strip of lining paper as a guide, exactly as you would for wallpaper – only mark down the wall instead of across it (see p. 32). Mark with a spirit level where the joins will come, providing a clear straight guide for hanging each piece across the wall.

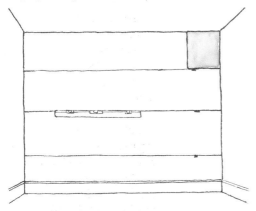

2. Paste up as described in Chapter 2, allowing for lengths that take you, if possible, across the full width of the wall. Hang the first piece starting at the top. Don't overlap the ceiling. Where you join ends together, these too will butt up to each other.

3. The next piece will butt up to the first piece across the wall. Work down the wall, turning the paper around the corners and smoothing it with the spatula as you work.

4. Work your way around the room, using your guides and butting up the edges. Trim off any excess at the skirting board with a metal ruler and craft knife.

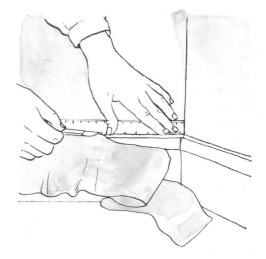

HINT
If the original wall surface was particularly poor and there are still indents showing after lining, they can be repaired with filler and sanded flat once it is dry.

Index

PICTURE CREDITS

Camera Press Limited 11, 13 (second left and middle), 16, 27, 55 (far left), 73 (far right), 75, 90 (second right), Martin Gent 76, Trevor Richards 37 (far right), 51 · IMS/Camera Press Limited 44, 54 (left), 55 (far right), 66, 69, 70, Kurt Hansson 62, Lucinda Symons 72 (right) · Elizabeth Whiting Associates 2 (top left, bottom left and right), 8 (left and right), 13 (far left, far right and second right), 15, 21, 23, 29, 37, 39, 40, 43, 47, 48, 52, 54 (left), 55 (middle left and right), 58, 61, 72 (left), 73 (second left), 79, 91 (left, middle and right), 93, 97, 101 · Harlequin 2 (top right), 9, 10, 105 (far left, left and right), 107, 108, 111, 112, 115, 116 · Osborne and Little 6, 105 (far right), 121 · The Stencil Store 12, 73 (far right), 80, 83, 84, 87, 88, 90 (left and right)